CONFLICTS

in the

COUNTRYSIDE

The New Battle for Britain

Professor David Bellamy, OBE

Shaw & Sons

Shaw's
Since 1750

Published by
Shaw & Sons Limited
Shaway House
21 Bourne Park
Bourne Road
Crayford
Kent DA1 4BZ

www.shaws.co.uk

© Shaw & Sons Limited 2005

Published May 2005

ISBN 0 7219 1670 8

A CIP catalogue record for this book is available from the British Library

Printed and bound in Great Britain by
Polestar Wheatons Limited, Exeter EX2 8RP

Contents

Picture Credits and Acknowledgement

Cover:
Illustration by Jenny Kingman
Artwork by Roy Sands

First colour section:
All pictures from the Royal Collection
The Royal Collection © 2005, Her Majesty Queen Elizabeth II

Second colour section:
Igor Beres – *Surfers*
Eric Bird, Red Alert – *Red squirrel*
Bourne Leisure Limited – *A Bellamy nature masterclass* and *The author and friends*
Chris Gomershall – *Abbotts Hall Farm*
Marek Nowakowski, Farmed Environment Company – *Conservation Grade farming*
Les Powell – *Heather moorland*
Roger H Smith – *Jellied eels*
Hans Stenstrom – *Red fox*
Nick Winchester – *Trout stream*

Acknowledgement
The publishers acknowledge the co-operation of Bourne Leisure Limited in the publication of this book.

About the Author

Professor David J Bellamy

OBE, BSc, PhD, Hon FLS, DSC, DUniv, CBiol, FIBiol, FCIWEM

Hon. Professor of Adult and Continuing Education, University of Durham; Special Professor of Geography, University of Nottingham; Hon. Professor of the University of Central Queensland.

President of The Conservation Foundation; The Wildlife Trusts Partnership; Plantlife International; WATCH; Coral Cay Conservation; National Association for Environmental Education; British Naturalists Association; Conservation Volunteers of Ireland; Galapagos Conservation Trust; British Institute of Cleaning Science; Association of Master Thatchers; British Home and Holiday Parks Association; Camping and Caravanning Club of Great Britain.

Vice President of British Trust for Conservation Volunteers; Fauna and Flora International; Marine Conservation Society; Australian Marine Conservation Society; Wild Trout Trust; Countrywide Holidays Association.

Trustee of the Living Landscape Trust; **Hon Fellow** of the Chartered Institute of Water and Environmental Management.

International consultant; **author** of 44 books; **writer** and **presenter** of some 400 television programmes on Botany, Ecology and the Environment.

Recipient of The Dutch Order of the Golden Ark; the UNEP Global 500 Award; The Duke of Edinburgh's Award for Underwater Research; BAFTA; Richard Dimbleby Award; BSAC Diver of The Year Award; RGS Busk Medal.

Chair of the international committee for the Tourism for Tomorrow Awards.

Originator, along with David Shreeve, of The Conservation Foundation and the Ford European Conservation Awards.

"A Cockney by extraction, I lived my formative years in wartime London. Tough kids in a tough environment in which I could pick a bunch of wild flowers for my mother on her birthday. VE day opened up the countryside to pedal power and the discovery of a wrap-around countryside replete with natural history of which small farms and game keepers were an integral part. Haslemere Educational Museum and the books of Arthur Ransome sowed the seeds of conservation and The Natural History Museum of Globetrotting. Although I desperately wanted to train in Classical Ballet, my only real talent was remembering the Latin names of plants. From that point on I never did a day's work; teaching at University was a case of learning with bright young minds out in the field and Auntie Beeb and ITV allowed me to discover the pearl in the oyster of the world. Rosemary and a large part-adopted multicultural family was the icing on the cake. All I want is 'Myocardial infarction' on my death certificate and a woodland burial."

PREFACE

In November 2002, the President of the Royal Society of Arts, His Royal Highness Prince Philip, called together a broad cross-section of wildlife, farming and conservation experts to discuss the problems facing the countryside. At the meeting, Prince Philip set out a Royal Challenge for everyone involved in conservation and countryside management to work together to recreate the 'balance of nature' in Britain. His Foreword can be found on page 13.

The rest of the book builds on the ideas and discussions that took place at the meeting and shows, with the help of much research and a variety of inspirational case studies, how such a vision might be achieved. It also shows that, in most cases, the main thing that has held up progress towards a solution is the intransigent attitude of those with extreme views, well stirred up by the media.

The case studies contain the good news from the battlefront. They prove that there is no need to reinvent any wheels, for what I like to call the 'Green Renaissance' is well under way. Each comes complete with a relevant web address so that you can find out more about what is going on at the 'battlefront' and how well the strategies are shaping up.

I hope that the book will help to lay to rest the main bones of this contention: the conflicts of interest, perception and ethics. It is my profound wish that the mud of intransigency on both sides will, in due time, become the clay of Britain's Green Renaissance.

The team that has made this part of the book possible are, in alphabetical order, Beverley Goodger, Robert Seaton and Rufus Bellamy and we would like to thank all the individuals and organisations that have freely given us so much help. Any mistakes or omissions are due to me, the oldest of the team, in whose style it is written.

David Bellamy

Foreword

By HRH The Duke of Edinburgh

The origins of this book go back to a series of conferences, organised by the RSA (Royal Society for the Encouragement of Arts, Manufactures and Commerce) in 1963, 1965 and 1970 under the title of 'The Countryside in 1970'. The object was to bring together the leaders of the public and private agencies, which had direct interests in, or direct influence on, the future of the British countryside, and the conservation of the natural environment. It was my contention then – it is still today – that the only hope of achieving the sort of countryside most people would like to see is by dialogue and cooperation between all these bodies.

Those conferences had three major consequences. In the first place, by bringing together the leaders of the major commercial, voluntary and statutory organisations they were able to meet and get to know each other personally. Secondly, they brought the whole issue of the conservation of nature to a much wider public. Finally they triggered the European Conservation Year of 1970 and then the United Nations Conference on the Human Environment in 1972.

Much has happened to both the human and the natural environments since the 1970s. Legislation intended to protect the natural environment has increased dramatically, but the natural system is seldom stable for long. While a number of introduced species and raptors have prospered, many native and migratory birds have declined. There can be little doubt that the encouragement of intensive agriculture by a regime of frequently inappropriate subsidies must take a big share of the blame, but I believe that our greatest problem is that, over recent years, the many older and more recently formed bodies involved in these issues seem to have grown apart again. There seems to be a mounting intolerance and lack of trust between factions. Instead of looking at the whole picture and trying to find compromise solutions, an increasing confrontation and antagonism seems to have developed between the various interests, all of whom should be on the same side.

It was with the hope of restoring dialogue and cooperation that I chaired a day-long conference at the RSA entitled 'The Balance of Nature, Land Management and Conservation' in November 2002. Everyone involved applauded the intention to protect the countryside, and to ensure the survival and welfare of wild species, and the outcome of the conference has convinced me that it is possible to arrive at rational solutions.

As a follow-up to the conference, David Bellamy and his team, have produced this important book. It sets out to explain the origins and nature of the conflicts, and details a whole series of cases where really successful conservation has been achieved through understanding and cooperation. I believe that they prove my contention that it is possible to reach satisfactory results by intelligent dialogue and sensible compromises arrived at by people with open minds and a sound knowledge, and understanding, of all the circumstances.

This book shows that unlikely partnerships of individuals, groups, businesses and communities of all sizes are now working together to achieve viable compromises between the many different interests, for the general benefit of rural society and the conservation of the natural environment.

Foreword

THE ROYAL CHALLENGE

by HRH Prince Philip

The origins of this book go back to a series of conferences, organised by the RSA (Royal Society for the Encouragement of Arts, Manufactures and Commerce) in 1963, 1965 and 1970 under the title of 'The Countryside in 1970'. The object was to bring together the leaders of the public and private agencies, which had direct interests in, or direct influence on, the future of the British countryside, and the conservation of the natural environment. It was my contention then – it is still today – that the only hope of achieving the sort of countryside most people would like to see is by dialogue and co-operation between all these bodies.

The conferences had three major consequences. In the first place, by bringing together the leaders of the major commercial, voluntary and statutory organisations they were able to meet and get to know each other personally. Secondly, they brought the whole issue of the conservation of nature to a much wider public. Finally they triggered the European Conservation Year of 1970 and then the United Nations Conference on the Human Environment in 1972.

Much has happened to both the human and the natural environments since the 1970s. Legislation intended to protect the natural environment has increased dramatically, but the natural system is seldom stable for long. While a number of introduced species and raptors have prospered, many native and migratory birds have declined. There can be little doubt that the encouragement of intensive agriculture by a regime of frequently inappropriate subsidies must take a big share of the blame, but I believe that our greatest problem is that, over recent years, the many older and more recently formed bodies involved in these issues seem to have grown apart again. There seems to be a mounting intolerance and a lack of trust between factions. Instead of looking at the whole picture and trying to find compromise solutions, an increasing confrontation and antagonism seems to have developed between the various interests, all of whom should be on the same side.

It was with the hope of restoring dialogue and co-operation that I chaired a day-long conference at the RSA entitled *The Balance of Nature, Land Management and Conservation*[1] in November 2002. Everyone involved applauded the intention to protect the countryside, and to ensure the survival and welfare of wild species, and the outcome of the conference has convinced me that it is possible to arrive at rational solutions.

As a follow-up to the conference, David Bellamy and his team have produced this important book. It sets out to explain the origins and nature of the conflicts, and details a whole series of cases where really successful conservation has been achieved through understanding and co-operation. I believe that they prove my contention that it is possible to reach satisfactory results by intelligent dialogue and sensible compromises arrived at by people with open minds and a sound knowledge, and understanding, of all the circumstances.

This book shows that unlikely partnerships of individuals, groups, businesses and communities of all sizes are now working together to achieve viable compromises between the many different interests, for the general benefit of rural society and the conservation of the natural environment.

---

[1] The full proceedings of the conference can be found on the internet at www.theRSA.org/balanceofnature

Chapter 1

ANSWERING THE CHALLENGE

GETTING THE BALANCE RIGHT

The royal gauntlet has been thrown down – a challenge to each and every one of us to help stitch Britain's once multicoloured and pleasant land back into better working order. The same Royal Challenge was made back in the post-flower power, pre-Greenpeace and Friends of the Earth days, 1970 to be exact. It certainly got all sides talking together, but sadly failed to stop the waves of environmental destruction that were, at that time, breaking over the countryside, courtesy of the much-flawed Common Agricultural Policy and other wrong-headed central planning.

Thirty years on and the challenge is more complex, our countryside is in far worse fettle and so is public understanding. We face a whole new set of problems brought about by changing demands and aspirations. Our urban masses live in concrete jungles built to accommodate cars, not communities of people; the countryside is out of reach and hence out of mind for many.

There are also now far fewer people working down on the farm, many aspects of rural life are in decay and there is much less understanding between townspeople and countryside folk over vital rural matters which affect us all. Yet, in essence, the challenge is still the same, to get all sides together to share their expertise and responsibilities as they restore, recreate and manage a vibrant living countryside on which they all depend and in which they live, work and play.

The rural battleground

The British Isles covers 94,475 square miles and is home to about 60 million of us. Innumerable acres of this land are wreathed in concrete,

15

tarmacadam and paving stones and plumbed for water, sewage, optic fibre, broadband and other services – the towns, cities and urban sprawl in which most of us live. The rest we'll call countryside – the bit that provides us with most of our water and a surprising amount of our food. It also services our population in other crucially important ways. It is an escape valve, used by a growing number of us to help relieve the pressures of modern life – a place for holidays, healthful exercise, adventure; in 'modspeak', a place in which to spend quality time.

Farmers, foresters, campers, caravanners, field sportspeople, climbers, hikers, horse riders, mountain bikers, hang-glider pilots, etc., etc. – the list of people who claim a 'stake' in the countryside grows all the time. Each has a different set of needs and desires for what is, sadly, a finite and shrinking resource; a rural pie that cannot be divided up infinitely.

Little wonder that the rural shires have become a battleground of different opinions shaken and stirred by the media. Headline after headline shouts the same thing about the countryside: What is the future of the countryside? Who is it there for? How should it be managed and looked after? No good news, just tension and disagreement about who calls the shots and who pays for the ammunition.

The sound of grinding axes

Most famously, these issues have galvanised the pro-countryside lobby to organise hundreds of thousands of country people to march peacefully on London, where they were picketed by those who think that some traditional forms of countryside management are 'cruel'. The recent scenes both outside and inside the Palace of Westminster have done little or nothing to solve the problem or to raise the profile of either our brand of governance or democracy in the eyes of the world.

However, arguments about countryside issues are being played out wherever you look: fat cat farms, chemical companies and supermarkets are cast as 'villains' by environmentalists, despite the fact that they help feed us all. Environmentalists are cast as enemies of 'cheap food' by the agricultural lobbyists, despite the fact that we all pay heavily to subsidise its present method of production. The wind farm brigade are hell-bent on spreading their turbines through some of the most beautiful parts of Britain, while the anti-wind farm brigade march up to the top of the hills they want to save, belayed by what they see as the real truth of the matter.

'Ramblers vs. landowners', 'Biotech companies vs. anti-GM campaigners', '4x4 drivers vs. the national parks', 'the rural poor vs. second home owners': this is anything but 'mellow fruitfulness' – it's war!

Such conflicts are not just between those with different ideologies or even those grinding different axes, they are keystone challenges facing our countryside. What, for example, are we going to do about the demands of tourism that are 'loving bits of it to death'? How can we fairly address the challenge that the need for mobility is producing roads just where nature does not need them? What are we to do about the fact that developers are building expensive homes in the rural shires that are out of reach of the young and poor of the countryside?

Losing touch with the countryside

Personally, I think that much of the problem comes down to the simple fact that many people have quite understandably lost touch with how the countryside works.

When I was young, we used to know how life worked in the raw. Rat and mouse-traps were important parts of house and garden furniture; short, sharp shock weapons that kept your food safe in those pre-refrigerator and Tupperware days. Flypapers were public gibbets displaying their writhing prey for all to see, not the pop of anonymous electrocution that today punctuates the background music in the delicatessen. Then butchers' shops displayed a cross-section of the edible birds of Britain fully feathered, ready for drawing and plucking, a necessary chore that was done on the kitchen table.

Half bullocks, lambs and pigs were hung in serried ranks to be quartered before your very eyes, butter was patted into saleable chunks and eggs came spattered with guano and feathers. Mums-to-be had babies at home and the whole family boiled the kettles and heard Mum and midwife at their labours. A grazed knee hurt, especially when iodine was applied and boils and carbuncles were lanced and treated with hot fomentations; while the dentist, lacking fast action drills and local anaesthetics, did it in the raw or used sick-provoking laughing gas. You got the cane at school – well, I did – and always tried not to cry.

I am not inferring that life was better in those days, but that even town-dwellers like me knew a lot more about how it all worked.

The Second World War exacerbated those experiences of life and death, something to be taken in your stiff upper lip stride, not a counsellor in sight except Mum and Gran who had seen it all before. It was in that tough world that I was brought up, in London, surrounded by a countryside that Winston Churchill considered to be "worth dying for". That is the reason I have been a campaigner for the wilder places and the wildflowers and wildlife they contain.

I was lucky, for I knew rural Britain as it was, worked by the joined-up thinking of everyday necessity. I also know that the same countryside is still there, waiting to be freed from the bondage of single issue vested interests and a media hell-bent on selling newsprint and airtime rather than using their clout to solve problems.

Pillories of misunderstanding

Sadly, in recent times the pillars of rural wisdom have become what are perhaps best described as the pillories of misunderstanding in an uncivil war of words. Here is a list of some of those most touted by the media:

- The perception that hunting mammals with dogs is cruel conflicts with the belief that it is the least cruel means of controlling pests or harvesting game.

- The conservation of game species for sport conflicts with the conservation of predators and raptors.

- The perception that animals have certain rights conflicts with the need to control pests at all levels in the food chain.

- The demand for water by humans conflicts with the survival of fish and their food supply.

- Subsidies for farmers and commercial fishermen conflict not only with the needs for the conservation of nature but with the demands of the market.

- The perception that killing animals for sport is unacceptable conflicts with the acceptance of the mass slaughter of domestic animals to be used as food for humans and their pets.

- Public access to sensitive conservation areas conflicts with the need of wild populations for peace and quiet, especially when breeding.

There are plenty more where these came from and every time I read them I see them in some new light, but they are the stuff single issue campaigns are made of.

Understanding the countryside

This war of words (and increasingly action) of course does little good for the countryside, where the continual erosion of quality green

19

space, peace and quiet, biodiversity and beauty goes on apace. So what can be done to meet the Prince's challenge, to accommodate everyone in a much-needed countryside renaissance?

As a scientist, my starting point in all this must be science. Sadly, that's something that has also got a pretty bad press over the years, but I believe that 'good science' is a powerful force for good. As you read through this book, you'll see time and time again that it is only with a full understanding of the 'science' of any situation that 'good' decisions can be made. This point was driven home recently when the results of a national trial of three genetically-modified crops – GM sugar-beet, GM maize and GM oil-seed rape – were published.

In a debate characterised by extreme views on both sides – GM crops are either 'Frankenfoods' or 'superfoods' depending on who you talk to – the results provided a firm foundation on which to base decision making. The research, which had taken over four years and involved over 280 trial fields, showed that two out of the three GM crops were worse for wildlife than their conventionally-bred counterparts. What was even more fascinating, however, was that the trials showed that there are other key factors that determine how wildlife-friendly a crop is. These are the types of herbicides used, the way they are used and, most interestingly of all, the crop itself. Maize, whether GM or not, turned out to be much worse for wildlife than either oil-seed rape or sugar-beet in the trials – a fact recognised by all farmers, ever since the first people of what we now call America planted this very demanding crop. That is why they always planted beans, a nitrogen fixer, alongside it, sowing the seeds of precision farming that carried the art and craft of organic agriculture forward across the centuries.

Informed decisions and actions

This kind of information is just what farmers (and the government) need if the countryside is to be put back into balance. The editor of

New Scientist trumpeted the importance of such good science: "The research proves that countries like Britain do not have to blow in the wind. They can use science to choose the level of farmland biodiversity they want and then set policies that reward farmers for adopting the practices that deliver it."

The GM-opponents, of course, say that none of the crops are safe because of potential gene-leakage, while the world still awaits economic proof that GM crops of any sort really benefit the farmer or the environment. There is also much writing on significant walls that even some of the big players are hedging their bets by investing in experiments on integrated crop management, a new form of precision farming, for after all their bottom-line business is selling farm chemicals.

As you will see in the chapter 'Down on the Farm', many farmers are already at work doing their own experiments to find out how best to manage their farms to encourage the maximum amount of wildlife. They are doing the 'good science' needed – practical science that could be applied across the country to turn our farmland from the silent wildlife desert that so much of it has become, into something that we and the birds can really sing about.

This process is not easy – it takes passion, commitment and hard work to construct a wildflower meadow, lay a hedgerow in the traditional manner, or plant and tend a native woodland. But it is a testament to the far-sightedness of many of Britain's front-line environmentalists – our best (and I use the word advisedly) farmers.

Of course, good science down on the farm is not worth a hill of organic beans if nobody will pay for the work of wildlife protection, management and restoration to take place. The good news is that, even here, there is a raft of solutions that together could succeed, bringing everyone involved in the food business – from the farmers and food processors, government and conservation groups, to the shops and consumers – to the round table of biodiversity and sustainability and keeping everyone, well almost everyone, happy.

Prejudice, misinformation and misunderstanding

Good science is one thing but it is no defence against prejudice, misinformation or misunderstanding. As I have said already, I believe that there is an information and understanding gap between those who work the countryside and those who don't. I hesitate to say between town and country, as there are many in the countryside, especially 'incomers' – like Linda Snell when she arrived in Ambridge – who know little of the day-to-day intricacies of its management.

This 'gap' has meant that the countryside's voice has not been heard properly on a whole range of issues – from the lack of facilities, housing, post offices, shops and employment that drive the young and poor out of the villages where they were born, to the role of the gamekeeper, hunter and recreational fishers in the management of the rural economy.

Because this latter issue has been made out to be the most contentious, at least by the lobbyists, let's take a look at it in a little more detail. Though an East Ender by abstraction, I have enjoyed the countryside for 70 years, studied it for 45 years and have lived in it for 30. I don't hunt, shoot or fish and so have had to think long and hard about the pros and cons of this side of countryside management. Luckily here, good science backed up by commonsense management practice that has been tried and tested over centuries comes to my rescue again and again when I've had to face the flak from both sides.

Think about this: rats, mice, pigeons, Canada geese, urban foxes and even feral dogs and cats have to be dealt with to keep the urban sprawl healthy and liveable. As a child, I had to help set the rat and mice traps and empty them when they had done their work. Most people living in towns today have this work done for them by the use of poison bait. This nationwide service performed by your local friendly pest controllers just about keeps the problem at bay. According to a National Pest Technicians Association's report, there was a 32% rise in the total number of brown rat infestations reported and dealt with by local authorities in the UK between 1998 and 2000. This is a vital service, a cull that goes on in most people's backyards day and night. The highly skilled technicians are out and about; thank God they come under little or no protest unless they don't turn up on time.

Standing up for countryside management

The same is sadly not true of those who perform the same vital jobs in our farms and in the broader countryside. Yet good farmers, gamekeepers and ghillies are key players in the balance of nature. They are also a police presence in the countryside in the war against badger-baiting, large-scale poaching, soil erosion and water pollution. To top it all, there are paying customers, and the sale of organic free-range game, fowl and fish help finance the whole affair.

Complex, isn't it? And how about this: statistics show that for every bird shot by a gun, about 99 are killed in a much less friendly way, by cats. How easy to redress the balance more in favour of our feathered friends, simply by keeping all cats in cages. Howls of derision, not only from cat lovers but also from those who would ask how many more rat and mice exterminators would be needed and who would pay for them? More owls, eagles, harriers and falcons in our countryside would certainly help to re-establish a more natural balance in this respect.

Add to this the positive environmental impact of gamekeeping. Without economically viable grouse shoots, much more of our uplands would have disappeared under acidifying alien conifers. Likewise, without well-managed lowland shooting estates, many more of our woodlands, hedgerows and flower-rich grasslands would have gone under the plough. It is time that the mainstream conservation groups all owned up to the fact that they have to control vermin in order to maintain the existence of the species their paid-up members expect to see when they visit their reserves. As I write, I am appalled to see that, although gamekeepers have been rightly fined for poisoning red kite, hen harrier and goshawk, no-one is being sued for chopping them up with wind turbines that indirectly help fund respected conservation bodies.

Things must be improved on all sides. Our Game Licence system is a sham, as it collects minuscule amounts of revenue and costs more to administer than it raises, and is widely ignored. If we followed the lead of our American cousins and made those who partake in field sports make their vital contribution to nature conservation in a direct and transparent way, we might just get each side to work together in an atmosphere of publicly shared trust.

Understanding, consensus and action

The importance of understanding and consensus in the countryside debate is, I hope, shown throughout the rest of this book, as is the vital role of teamwork and partnership – a way of working that, by its very nature, depends on people all pulling in the same direction.

This fact has been acknowledged by the development of so-called BAPs. Now, to you and me, baps are flat, elliptical bread rolls that are still a delicious part of breakfast in the north of England and Scotland: the stuff bacon butties are made of. So good are they that they are now sold across Britain. However, to a conservationist, they are Biodiversity Action Plans. Fortunately these too are now nationwide, schemes that set priorities for nationally and locally important habitats and wildlife. They have, at least, focused the attention of many disparate conservation groups on the plight of individual species and habitats. To wildlife, they are just as good as a butty is to a hungry Northerner and they are vital to the well-being of the countryside.

BAPs are already helping to form the bedrock of wildlife conservation in the UK and, like the rest of the projects highlighted in this book, show that there are many truly amazing things already going on to help solve the problems and win the battle. Most are common sense but some are really wild ideas that have been proven to work. Sadly, good news rarely makes the headlines and jealousy often clouds even the greenest of issues, so much so that the general public remains ill-informed about the real problem, let alone the real progress that is being made.

As you read on, you'll see that many positive projects have come about because of enlightened self-interest; for example, tourism businesses realising that the best way to ensure that their guests enjoy their stay in the countryside (and return to spend more money) is to play their part in maintaining and improving the quality of that countryside experience. I hope that you'll also get a feeling for the commitment and passion of all those people who really stick their necks out and do something for the countryside.

This book aims to help you find your way around the countryside – both practically and metaphorically – to understand what's happened to it, how it 'works' (or doesn't) and hopefully to see that there are lots of ways forward. It focuses on the main areas of contention and misunderstanding to show that, once we get beyond the rhetoric, progress can be made.

Overall, I hope that this book shows that the "present atmosphere of prejudice, mistrust and hostility" can be and is being dispelled and that "the public arguments about single issues" can be and are being brought "back to intelligent and tolerant discussion" – and, of course, that it will lead to more positive action on all sides.

The time has surely come for us to rediscover the roots of the environmental movement. These were simply the conservation of the local diversity of nature that used solar power to cleanse water, make and keep the soil fertile, reduce, reuse and recycle all the raw materials and was able to heal catastrophes and turn every new opportunity to advantage.

It is my considered opinion, after more than 50 years' work as an ecologist and over 40 on the conservation campaign trail, that sustainable redevelopment means working with nature as far as possible. To quote the words of Karl Linnaeus who allowed the natural historians of the world to name the names of all living things in a heritage language that became the common tongue of science: "Nature's economy shall be the base of our own, for it is immutable, ours is secondary" [Linnaeus 1763]. That is what this book is all about.

This book is for you – a person who enjoys and uses the countryside – whether you are a landowner, tenant, walker, rambler, caravanner, shootist, fisher or just someone who enjoys the wonder of it all from the window of a car, train or tour bus. I hope that, once you've finished reading, you will join the great partnership that is already stitching our countryside back into good heart. Remember, the Prince's Challenge includes you!

Chapter 2

THE MAKING OF OUR COUNTRYSIDE

LESSONS FROM HISTORY

The most amazing thing about the British countryside is that only 12,000 years ago all of it was just starting to emerge from the grip of an ice age and, since then, all of it has felt the touch of human endeavour. After the ice had shaped the land, hunters, farmers and foresters came into conflict with nature in the raw, changing the landscapes as they tamed them in order to make a livelihood for their families.

To understand how best to manage the British countryside, we therefore need to know how it was created. We need to understand the many different factors that came together to give us the scenery and the native plants and animals we so cherish today. So, let us look back through 14,000 years of interglacial British history, using evidence unearthed by pollen analysis, archaeology and written records, to find out how the British Isles came to be like they are today.

As you read through, take a look at how the temperature changed. As you'll see from post-glacial history, real global warming had already begun as an almost unpopulated Britain emerged from the ice, long before humans began the wholesale burning of fossil fuels. Many well-informed people are asking the following pertinent question: is the latest round of ups and downs in our far-from-temperate climate due to burning fossil fuel, are we still in the grip of the ups and downs of the last ice age, or is it a bit of both?

The last ice age, or was it? (14,000 BP – Before Present)

14,000 years ago, Britain was no more than a bulge on the north-western edge of what we now call Europe, a great chunk of real estate that was enduring yet another ice age. This most recent period of global cooling had begun 60,000 years earlier. As the polar ice-caps expanded to their maximum extent, areas north of the Bristol Channel and the Wash were warped under billions of tons of crushing, gouging ice, sculpting the underlying rocks into the peaks, valleys and plains we now know. This hard landscaping shaped the ground upon which the British countryside would develop over the next 14,000 years.

Glacial meltdown (14,000 to 12,000 BP)

Somewhere between 14,000 and 12,000 years ago, the climate of north-western Europe entered a warm-up phase and the polar ice-caps began to melt. This marked the start of an interglacial period. Such cycles of global cooling and warming have occurred approximately every 100,000 years, due in part to cyclical changes in both the shape of the earth's orbit round the sun and the tilt of the earth's axis.

At present, we could be in an interglacial era, which means that this warm period could last for tens of thousands of years. However, as with previous interglacial periods, our climate could flip back into the freezer – a chilling thought!

12,000 years ago, the landscape, freed from ice, was bitterly cold and dry. With so much fresh water still locked away in ice-caps or permafrost, the sea-level was probably as much as 400 feet lower than it is today. That's why Britain was joined to Europe and Ireland, so it was possible for hardy animals to walk in once there were plants for them to eat.

At that time, Britain was treeless and its newly-forming soils were rapidly colonised by plants that today are at home in the arctic tundra or on the tops of our highest mountains or rocky ledges – grasses, sedges and low-growing shrubs – sparse vegetation but enough to feed herds of migratory animals.

Although most of Europe's early Stone Age people at that time preferred the shelter of the cave systems of southern France and Spain, art has recently been discovered in caves in Creswell Crags in Derbyshire dating from 12,500 years ago; positive proof that an estimated 400 to 500 souls were hardy enough to extend their hunting trips even into the icy wastes of England, where reindeer, giant elk and even mammoth were on the menu. These were the first ancient Brits to feel the effects of global warming.

The return of the trees (12,000 to 7,500 BP)

As the ice caps continued to melt, conditions became more suitable for tree growth. The climate-induced changes in vegetation are recorded in the pollen grains preserved in the peaty wetlands that were growing at that time. Most plants produce distinctive pollen or spores which can be identified under the microscope of modern science, telling us an amazingly detailed story. It was not all plain warming; a cold snap called the Alerod Oscillation caused the plants to die and the animals to retreat south into warmer climes. However, within 5,000 years of becoming free from ice, trees had repopulated much of Britain, at first hardy species such as juniper, birch and willow, then hazel and pine, joined by oak, elm and alder and finally ash, beech and lime.

The growing population of Middle Stone Age (Mesolithic) hunters and gatherers (eventually an estimated 10,000), vying to make a living in Britain, must have wondered where all the trees were coming from and where the next meal was going to come from. These people were not farmers; they browsed wild fruits, nuts and seeds, gathered shellfish and hunted wild animals, birds and fish to give them the meat, skins, bones and sinews they needed to survive. Their technologies of flint and bone were simple and they lived at the mercy of their environment.

As more and more of Britain became covered with scrub and

woodland, it was no longer easy to spot a slow-moving herd of mammoth from afar, while the enormous antlers of the giant elk made their escape ever more difficult through the trees. Eventually, both headed for the wall of extinction as the climate and the balance of nature changed.

Britain becomes an island (7,500 BP)

Global warming continued, melting glaciers and returning water to the sea via clouds and rain. Rising sea-levels finally cut Britain off from mainland Europe about 7,500 years ago, isolating its populations of plants, animals and Mesolithic people from the rest of the Continent. The so-called native membership of Britain's flora and fauna was now fixed and species that hadn't yet spread back to Britain from the warmer south were barred from this exclusive hunting, fishing and natural history club, unless they had the means to cross the English Channel. Travel within Britain was also being made ever more difficult, as the trees took over the land and there were fewer and fewer places where the plants and animals of open ground could survive. Fantastic forests yes, but otherwise and in biodiversity terms it was a somewhat boring landscape in which open ground and distant views were a rarity.

In competition with an increasing density of trees and people, the reindeers, elk, wild ox, boar, brown bear, beaver and European lynx present in Britain's woodlands at this time all gradually headed for extinction. The ox survived into Celtic times as it had ritual significance for Celts. Some people believe that the demise of wild boars, inveterate grubbers-up of everything, left Britain with a legacy not shared by the rest of Europe, namely our bluebell woods.

Britain gets wetter (7,500 to 4,400 BP)

As temperatures rose, producing summer temperatures up to three degrees Celsius higher than those experienced in Britain today, more water evaporated from the sea, increasing rainfall. Water vapour, the main greenhouse gas, was in abundance, its presence in the atmosphere trapping the heat of the day. In this warmer and wetter Britain, wetlands began to spread, swamping trees as bogs developed in every hollow where water and sediment could accumulate. These were welcome open spaces for game, people and plants alike. The sun-loving pioneering plants that had first colonised the land as the ice disappeared had been pushed out, surviving only where the trees could not grow. These new open spaces allowed some of them to regain their old territories, and further help was at hand on a massive scale.

Some of the 50,000 or so New Stone Age (Neolithic) immigrants who occupied Britain at this time had already discovered the delights of the Lake District, one of which was a very useful sort of hard greenstone from the Langdale Pikes. They soon learned to polish this, producing axe heads sharp enough to chop down oak trees. They even exported this very useful bit of kit far and wide to mainland Europe. Not quite a chainsaw but trees could now be felled with greater ease.

This was just what the Neolithic immigrants needed, for they were farmers and they required open land on which to grow their crops and graze their domesticated animals. Many of the flowers that used to grow in those same areas at the end of the ice age returned to grace the open fields, pastures, heaths and trackways. This made Britain much easier to make a living from and to travel about in. The felled timber was useful for all sorts of things, including permanent huts, villages and stockades to protect animals from wolves, foxes, bears and other predators.

Britain basks in a warm, dry spell (4,400 to 2,750 BP)

Felling, grazing and burning were important Neolithic land management practices for they removed and kept the trees at bay. If the chopping stopped, the trees, woodland plants and wild animals would soon return. However, in the most densely populated parts of Britain, such management appears to have produced more permanent change, resulting in the formation of the famous Brecklands of Norfolk and other heath and grassland areas, some of which persist to this day. So it was that these, our first settled farmers, began to create and manage the more diverse landscapes we enjoy today.

As technology progressed from stone to metal, the process of change speeded up. Neolithic quarries and Bronze Age copper and tin mines pockmarked the landscape, providing the first 'brownfield sites', perfect havens for the plants and animals that thrive in open places.

Life must have been good at this time for field patterns and ever larger settlements, burial sites and monuments appeared on the scene. Britain's Bronze Age climate was a warm and pleasant one as its population crossed the half million mark. Together all these people produced and managed a patchwork of habitats, cropping the products of pastures, meadows and grasslands while hunting and gathering in forests and other wilder bits – new complex landscapes bursting with biodiversity.

Blanket peat begins to spread (2,750 to 1,960 BP)

Bronze gave way to iron as Britain's island race really got a good reason to start complaining about the weather. It became colder and wetter, rising water-tables encouraged wetlands to expand and acid peat bogs began to cover more and more of our upland areas. The resulting blanket peat swamped any birch and pine that still grew there, forming vast tracts of peaty moorland. Cloaked in heather, these supported red deer, golden eagle, grouse, black cock, golden plover and many other birds, insects and plants that to this day make these open, windswept areas their home.

Petrified birch and pine roots, stumps and even whole trees preserved in the peat bear witness to this massive shift in the balance of nature, brought about in part by the changeable climate of our islands.

At this time, Iron Age settlers in the colder, wetter uplands of the north and west were pastoral farmers, whose herds of cattle provided them with their staple diet of meat and milk. In the drier, warmer south and east, arable farming methods were developing apace and with them came another burst of new biodiversity.

Iron ploughs, chalk, manure and the practice of leaving fields fallow following a period of cultivation allowed extensive harvesting of cereals. The plants and animals that had returned to these now open places found more permanent homes and many new imports joined them. Britain could by then begin to boast about one of its most colourful spectacles, the multicoloured cornfield, replete with hosts of nectar-full flowers, hordes of bees producing honey and other insects feeding the flocks of little birds (whose numbers were in turn kept in balance by birds of prey (raptors)), with red kites clearing up the mess.

Smelting all the iron required lots of charcoal and so the management of woodlands changed to produce enough small logs for charcoal burners. This required the cutting of woodlands at regular intervals and was called coppicing. It not only produced a sufficiency of charcoal but an ever-shifting cycle of sun and shady habitats in which a diversity of plants, insects and animals could find a home. The vast majority of the one million Celts of Iron Age Britain lived as settled farmers in a patchwork of biologically and agriculturally diverse landscapes.

The Romans arrive (40 to 410 AD)

The Romans, who settled amongst the Celtic tribes, not only tried to teach them Latin but also built on their agricultural practices, extending the cultivation of cereals into the fenland and those more favourable parts of upland Britain that they had managed to occupy. In the lowlands, they introduced new crops such as plums, figs, vines, walnuts, mulberry, medlar, peas and radishes, as well as herbs such as dill and fennel. They also introduced other new plants to the British flora. Some, such as ground elder, were brought on purpose to be used as potherbs, while others were stowaways hitching a ride amongst the grain imported to feed the mighty Roman army. Corn marigolds and corncockles came this way, adding to the annual cornfield spectacle that already included cornflowers.

The Roman obsession with engineering straight roads to speed their economy presented all the cornfield annuals with hundreds of miles of open ground along which they could gain a foothold. So they began to spread, travelling rapidly to pastures new, all set about by Roman towns with their markets for food and other produce. The land and the buoyant economy could now support around five to six million people. One favourite pastime of the Romans was to drink wine made from grapes grown as far north as York; another was to hunt brown bears, hastening their extinction.

The Dark Ages (410 to 700 AD)

The Roman Army left in 410 AD. The vision, energy and wealth that had produced a network of urban centres, supported by extensive agriculture, deserted these shores too. Towns were depopulated and the majority of people reverted to subsistence level farming. Some cultivated land went back to scrub and woodland. Many farms on upland chalk were abandoned, leaving the ground clear for beech trees to establish themselves, perhaps paving the way for Britain's oaks to make a comeback.

Meanwhile, some of the lower-lying fenland that had helped fill the Roman breadbasket was claimed back by nature as the sea-level along the south-east coast appeared to rise, flooding large tracts of eastern England. In fact, what was actually happening was that the whole of the south of England was sinking due to a eustatic rebound, a natural process that is continuing today. The enormous weight of ice that had pressed down, especially on Scotland, was gone and the earth's crust was heaving a sigh of relief. Scotland began to rise and the south of England got more than a sinking feeling.

Anglo-Saxon and Viking invasions (410 to 1066 AD)

The simple ploughs used by Celts and Romans alike were only effective at turning lighter soils, thus those areas with heavy clay soils, including many of our lowland river valleys, escaped cultivation and their trees remained. This was all to change with the arrival of the Anglo-Saxons in the fifth century AD. Their heavy ploughs pulled by oxen made light work of these valley soils, and down came the trees, in went the crops and Anglo-Saxon place names – -ham and -ton – spread throughout lowland England.

Their subsistence farmsteads with straight-sided acre-strips formed the basis for the later development of the mediæval open field system. The feudal system brought peasant farmers and landlords to a state of uneasy dependency that endured for many centuries. The Anglo-Saxons were not quite as successful in upland Britain, where few of their place names exist. Here the Celtic landscapes remained unchanged until Norwegian Vikings settled the valleys in these areas in the ninth and tenth centuries.

Between 600 AD and 1100 AD, European organic agriculture entered its golden age and the Vikings rose to prominence. Greenland, now a frozen wasteland, was then an outpost of Viking civilisation, though not for long. Our climate took a turn for the worse, as King Canute (1016–1035) had to dig peat from the fens to keep his people warm.

The Middle Ages – the Domesday Book and all that (1066 to 1536 AD)

William the Conqueror's Domesday Book of 1086 provides a unique and fastidious record of who owned what land across England and parts of Wales. The feudal system was well and truly enforced and villagers were easily evicted, mere tenants whose fortunes changed at the whim of their overlords.

Royal hunting forests, most of them containing great tracts of open land, were given legal protection and many tenants were evicted from their homes, so that the arable land that they tended could revert to 'wastes' to improve the cover for the Royal game. With the Normans also came the rabbit, tended by warreners; a tasty delicacy throughout the Middle Ages and a pest ever since that has needed constant culling. Here was a source of organic free-range food that lasted until the middle of the twentieth century when myxomatosis took it off the menu.

In the mid-twelfth century, the Cistercians founded about 50 monasteries. They were efficient farmers and estate managers, and their detailed written records show how wealthy sheep farmers and wool merchants could become. Vast areas of woodland in the north of England were cleared for sheep pasture, while many of Britain's remaining oak woods were managed as 'coppice with standard'. This meant that a certain number of oak trees were allowed to grow to maturity among the resprouting coppice stools. During their life they provided nesting sites and bat roosts, their timber eventually being used for special building jobs that reached up to heaven. This and the much more regular supply of smaller logs and poles ensured a more sustainable living for woodmen, woodland owners and woodland wildlife alike.

Outside the woods, crops were grown in open fields, where strip agriculture produced the ridge and furrow pattern still visible in some fields to this day. Biodiversity increased as two fields out of three bore a crop, while the third field lay uncultivated, or fallow, for 12 months.

Most of the population lived and worked in the countryside and it was during this time that our familiar picture-postcard landscape of villages, each clustering around a church and village manor-house and farm, began to appear. The countryside surplus was traded to the townsfolk who developed new crafts, skills and trades that were sustained by, and contributed to, a buoyant economy.

By 1300, the population of Britain had grown to seven million – double its size only 200 years before, and Britain's agricultural system began to feel the strain. The three-year field system was sometimes stretched to ten years of continuous cultivation and marginal land was enlisted for agricultural purposes in an attempt to keep food supply apace with demand. Uplands, heathlands, marshlands, fens and woodlands were turned back to farming and hedgerows became increasingly common to define coveted acres of productive land.

As in any boom situation, disaster was around the corner. Rain-induced harvest failure caused a seven-year famine, which was followed by the Black Death from 1348 to 1350. Britain's population was halved and whole communities were wiped out. By the 1400s, much of the marginal land that had been brought under cultivation had reverted to scrub, moorland and pasture and the fortunes of Britain's rural economy had come full circle. It was once again dependent upon sheep farming and wood production, despite 200 years of attempting to increase agricultural output.

Tudors and Stuarts (1536 to 1714 AD)

Britain's Tudor and Stuart period heralded a renaissance in art, science and literature that accompanied the growth of towns. Timber was needed for wooden ships, buildings and for smelting even more iron ore, and the consequent pressure on our woodlands continued apace. It was during this time that the last wolf-packs were being exterminated. The only large members of our woodland fauna left were roe and red deer. The latter moved up into the open hill country where poor grazing gradually reduced their stature.

Agriculture now occupied nearly all suitable soils, but improvements in yield were limited by the availability of land and manure. Manure depended on flock size which, in turn, was limited by the amount of food that could be used to feed the sheep during the winter. As there was little food to spare, the only way around the problem for most farmers was to slaughter them in the autumn.

In the seventeenth century, farmers learned to use red and white clover as a nitrogen-fixing crop, which reduced the need for manure and provided a welcome boost to soil fertility. In turn, this boosted bees and honey production, maintaining productivity and supporting a steady British population of 5.7 million. To put it all into perspective, our population today is more than ten times that number. It was during this period that even the mighty River Thames froze over, enough to allow oxen to be roasted on its solid waters, thanks to the so-called 'Little Ice Age'. At the same time, hurricane-force winds blew the roofs off houses, opening them up to the wrath of the heavens. Indeed, records of plant and animal remains on the seabed indicate that this was just one of six such cold snaps that affected the balance of nature in Britain.

The Agricultural Revolution (1750 to 1850 AD)

Whether an agricultural revolution actually took place is still debated but from 1750 onwards something must have happened to increase the amount of food available. The population began to grow rapidly, almost tripling in the next 100 years, and agricultural output expanded with it.

During this time, the subsistence farming that had supported the population for 6,000 years was replaced by a farming industry that allowed regional specialisation. Britain became a net exporter of food, as winter fodder (in the form of turnips) allowed stock to be slaughtered throughout the winter and fresh meat to be available throughout most of the year.

Enclosure of land, including woodland, increased and many landlords conserved and extended tree cover on their lands by excluding livestock and planting oak, ash, beech and Scots pine. Sycamore and larch, introduced to Britain during the sixteenth and seventeenth centuries, also spread freely during this period, as the role of woodland as a provider of timber and coppice declined and its value as an amenity and as an emblem of social status increased.

Improved agricultural productivity and efficiency meant that more food was produced per worker and, by 1850, only about one-fifth of Britain's workforce remained in agriculture, the smallest proportion of any country in the world at this time. Despite this, in 1850 Britain could still produce 80% of the food needed by its increasingly urban population, thanks solely to 100 years of organic agricultural intensification.

The Industrial Revolution and beyond (1850 to 1901 AD)

By 1851, Britain had established itself as the world's leading industrial power and half of its 21 million people lived in towns. The expanding industries and their supporting services employed four-fifths of its workforce, while the rural few did their best to feed this, the world's first urban nation.

Canals, railways and roads provided a transport infrastructure that could move food, raw materials and people long distances in short periods of time. The value of the local food trade dwindled, as national and international markets opened up to supply the fast-growing towns and cities with an increasing diversity of foods. The driving force behind all this expansion, migration and social change was coal, not wood. No wonder the bulk of the urban population was becoming ever more detached from the countryside upon which it had once been completely dependent.

The value of Britain's ancient wool industry, mainstay of the rural economy since the Middle Ages, declined as cotton, imported from plantations in the United States, replaced wool as the fibre of choice in the coal-guzzling, steam-powered mills of Lancashire and Yorkshire. Dependency on fossil fuel was no longer confined to the town and city-based industries, as farming began to depend upon chemical fertilisers and steam-driven machinery.

By 1901, three-quarters of Britain's population of 37 million souls lived in towns, enduring the problems caused by acid rain and smog. This depopulation of Britain's rural landscape was speeded by poor harvests at home and the import of cheap wheat – 75% of all we needed – available by the shipload from the prairies of North America.

Meanwhile, Britain's urban population continued to lose touch with the countryside, which became viewed by some through dewy eyes as a curious romantic idyll. This image was popularised by poets and writers such as William Wordsworth and Beatrix Potter, while others vilified the countryside as the inaccessible property of wealthy landowners, fat cats of industry included.

World Wars (1914 to 1945 AD)

By 1910, 80% of Britain's population lived in towns or cities and, at the outbreak of the First World War, Britain's farmers were only producing one-third of the food that supported its population of 42 million. In an attempt to restore a modicum of self-sufficiency, the British government encouraged the nation to "Dig for Victory". This brought several million acres of land back into food production and included the massive planting of onions and other herbal medicines. Sphagnum moss was collected from our peat lands for use as wound dressings in the trenches and forestry was revitalised to produce pit props.

This was a time of invasions and, as battle raged on the western front, imported grey squirrels, sika deer and mink were all establishing themselves in a landscape where abundant food and the absence of their natural predators would allow them to shift the balance of nature in their favour.

After that terrible war, the Forestry Commission was set up to develop state forests on land deemed unsuitable for agriculture. This smothered acre upon acre of Britain's open moorlands with an impenetrable thatch of alien conifers that would grow rapidly, even in the poor soils shunned by our native timber trees. The scale of the operation and our wet climate was good for the softwood merchants but had dire effects on the biodiversity and integrity of these long, treeless landscapes and the ecology of the rivers that flowed from them.

What is more, pre-Beeching railways and the advent of the family car fuelled the demand of the urban masses to get away for a day or more in what I still like to call the *Swallows and Amazons Forever* countryside – a countryside immortalised in the pages of Arthur Ransome's bestsellers that included much about children doing their best to save the birds of our countryside.

Apart from common land, most of the countryside that surrounded the still-expanding urban centres was privately owned, and attempts by the public to gain access to it brought the landowners and the would-be land users head to head.

Public interest groups that were formed during this period lobbied the government for measures to protect and allow access to the countryside for the benefit of everyone. Escalation of the conflict continued and, following the mass trespass on Kinder Scout in 1932, a standing committee of voluntary sector organisations was set up to put pressure on the government to resolve the situation.

Boring, boring it may seem but it was of immense importance for, in May 1936, the Standing Committee on National Parks was formed. Its role was to persuade the government that National Parks would provide the solution to what appeared to be an intractable problem.

Despite the Second World War (when the Women's Land Army was drafted in to help feed a nation short of 50,000 farmworkers, which certainly helped and gave many townies a glimpse of how good and bad life down on the farm could be), the work of the Committee continued, culminating in the 1949 National Parks and Access to the Countryside Act. Britain's urban population could, at last, officially re-establish contact with its rural roots.

Modern Britain – CAP in hand (1945 to present)

Britain's Second World War reconstruction heralded a new agricultural revolution that reached its peak of intensity in the 1980s. This was a war on the landscape that grazed, ploughed and polluted its way into the history books as the most destructive phase of British land management in its 10,000-year history.

Industrial pollution also took its toll on the countryside. Although the effects of acid rain were claimed by some to be green wash, the acidification of streams, rivers and lakes by sulphur dioxide pouring from giant power-stations and homely grates alike did tremendous damage to the invertebrates that feed our freshwater fish. This was in addition to the damage that had already been done by those serried ranks of conifers still being planted in our uplands. Implementation of the Clean Air Act saw the last London smog in 1952 and cut down on one source of acid in the rain (and also the supply of free sulphur fertiliser to all farmers except those downwind from coal-burning power-stations).

Meanwhile, mechanisation of the agricultural industry increased yields and decreased the number of farms and farmworkers as Britain again attempted to restore its agricultural self-sufficiency. When Britain joined the European Economic Community in 1972, its farmers became strait-jacketed by a Common Agricultural Policy that rewarded production with subsidies – whether the produce was needed or not.

Farming in the 1970s and 1980s became an industry in the same boat as the coal and steel industries at that time; they could only stay afloat as long as they were heavily subsidised by tax-payer's hard-earned cash. No-one wanted to see farming disappear from Britain and few farmers could refuse the temptation of a Eurostar gravy train that meant the more you grew the more you earned.

Hedgerows and woodlands were grubbed out, ponds were drained and ancient grassland and heathland soils were ploughed for the first time to accommodate monocultures of chemically-cosseted crops. In the race for subsidised profit, fertilisers were used so freely that nutrients flowed into watercourses, encouraging the growth of micro-organisms that used up all the oxygen, resulting in dead fish and stinking rivers. This, the scourge of eutrophication, was not helped by the increased stock densities that CAP subsidies funded. Ever-deepening slurry pits leaked their nutrient-rich ooze into rivers and, as mutton gave way to lamb, stock levels became so dense that grazing pressure further upset the balance of our uplands, so much so that unpalatable bracken, mat grass and hard rush seized the advantage, invading ever-larger areas.

Thanks to the CAP, the five decades of destruction that followed the Second World War saw Britain lose 99% of its lowland heath, 80% of its chalk downland, 80% of its fens and mires, 50% of its ancient lowland woods, 90% of its lowland ponds and 50% of its hedgerows. Any idea of balance went out of the window as thousands of small farmers who could no longer make a living left the land; so the big boys moved in, buying their land and raking in the subsidies. All this occurred as butter mountains, milk lakes and grain intervention stores made the headlines that rubbed in the fact that the tax-payers were footing the bill.

Little wonder that Britain's now almost totally urban population lost sympathy with agriculture, let alone rural attitudes. Farmers came to be viewed by many as over-subsidised vandals of the countryside who had failed in their duty to protect our beloved rural landscape. Meanwhile, those private landowners who had throughout this carnage successfully maintained the balance of huge tracts of Britain, deriving some income from hunting, shooting and fishing, were vilified for denying the public access to their lands.

However, some warnings did not go unheeded, like the one against the extensive use of pesticides containing deadly mixtures of phosphorous and chlorine. They were very efficient at killing all insects – both the baddies and goodies – but they also killed other much larger creatures at the top of the food chain. Some of our raptors began to produce eggs with very thin shells, with dire consequences during incubation. Rachel Carson's book *Silent Spring* so frightened the chemical companies that they began to invest millions of pounds developing alternative chemicals that targeted the real problems rather than the high-flying bystanders. Since then our raptor numbers have been climbing, causing problems to the balance of our bird life in other ways. However, sadly there are still some very poisonous chemicals in everyday use.

The BSE crisis further diminished public confidence in British agriculture and then another catastrophe struck; huge areas of rural Britain were quarantined in a futile attempt to stop the spread of foot and mouth disease. The end looked nigh. The only good news was that, as the result was so devastating, it opened more than a few closed minds to the commonsense truth of the matter: a balanced approach to the management of our countryside is of crucial importance.

Many lessons were learnt from the cruel blow dealt to rural Britain by the foot and mouth epidemic of 2001, but two stand out. These are that agriculture shapes the face of the British countryside and the majority of British people consider the countryside to be a national public asset. What a challenge! How is the life of the countryside to be maintained? Who will pay for it? How can we ensure that Britain's countryside has a sustainable future?

Thank God all is not lost, there are still many forgotten corners of these islands that are forever England, Scotland, Wales and Northern Ireland. Here, great partnerships are at work laying down firm foundations for a green renaissance that could blossom across the length and breadth of the UK. What better time for a right Royal Challenge?

Chapter 3

OUR UPLANDS

WELL-WORN WILDERNESS OR PLENTEOUS SOLITUDE

Starting at the top: our uplands are very special, a backdrop where storm-clouds gather and the first snows of winter remind us that another year is drawing to a close. For most of us to stand atop Ben Nevis, Snowdon or Scafell is as much of an achievement as tackling Everest which, incidentally, now costs you about $1,000 just for the entrance fee and needs whole parties of willing volunteers to follow on to clean up the mess.

So, just how valuable are Britain's hills, moors, crags, mountains, valleys and dales to people? For a start, their beautiful and dramatic landscapes provide much of the water for most of our rivers, aquifers and hence for us. They also provide livelihoods and homes for some and quality space and time for others.

But it takes only a cursory look at the situation in Britain's uplands to realise that things are not all rosy. In many places, the millions of people who retreat to the hills from the urban lowlands are unintentionally destroying the very resource they seek, while the interests of nature conservation often seem at odds with the needs of the people who live, work and relax in our mountains and hills. Does it have to be like this?

Co-operation on Stanage Edge

Stanage Edge lies in the middle of one of the most popular and heavily used rock-climbing areas in Britain – the Peak District National Park. Despite the 500,000 picnickers, walkers, climbers, hang-gliders, paragliders and potholers who use the area, two pairs of one of Britain's rarest and most endangered birds, the ring ouzel, are given the space and privacy they need to breed. The magic ingredient in this recipe for success is teamwork between people who could all too easily be adversaries. By working together, the members of the Stanage Forum have been able to improve their understanding of what ring ouzels and people want from the area, and to explore and agree ways of helping both (see page 61).

The success at Stanage Edge shows how involvement, communication and participation (in other words teamwork), mutual understanding and respect win the day. It shows that, given collaboration and restraint by all parties, public access to sensitive conservation areas need not conflict with the requirements of wild populations for peace and quiet – particularly in the breeding season. The project proves that it is possible to manage an area for the benefit of people and wildlife. Can this be a universal truth? Let's take a look at our heather moorlands.

75% of the world's remaining heather moorland is found in Britain, where it has been an important part of the landscape for over 6,000 years. Home to a very special range of plants, birds and insects, it is one of the world's rarest habitats, much rarer than the much-talked-about tropical rainforest. What a responsibility! Surely, as a first world country, we should look after it?

The late summer haze of purple beloved by tourists and bees alike was created, and is still maintained, by managed, controlled burning and what used to be controlled grazing. In the old days, the moors were stinted, which meant that the number of sheep were limited by mutual consent – or a punch-up in the pub. In some areas, where upland agriculture has become uneconomical, grouse shooting is now the key source of revenue generation to support the local economy and keep the moorlands free from trees.

All this involves a quite complex pattern of management. In the winter when many of the birds have gone, most plants are dormant and invertebrates are safe underground, mosaics of small patches of heather are carefully burned. When done properly, this provides billions of succulent new heather shoots to feed grouse chicks, lambs and insects, including honeybees, while providing fire breaks in the older, leggy heather which gives shelter from the wind for lambs and birds alike. From spring through to summer, a controlled density of sheep may graze safely and red grouse and a multitude of other birds raise their free-range young. This management technique gives us the moorland scenes that so many people treasure. If the uplands were left to Mother Nature, a long struggle would ensue as a mix of woodland tried to reassert itself. This would not only change the whole aspect of the uplands but also make access and fire control ever more difficult.

Gamekeeping under fire

Unfortunately, the traditional methods of rotational burning and predator control used to manage heather moorlands for the red grouse have provoked some angry confrontations. "Keeper fined over rare bird death" (*BBC News*, 25/05/2001); "Gamekeepers accuse RSPB of harassment" (*The Sunday Times*, 12/10/2003) are just a couple of headlines from recent years.

Such confrontations are a far cry from the co-operation that is helping the ring ouzels of Stanage Edge. It's the health of three-quarters of the world's heather moorland that's at stake, so why are the should-be team members involved in this vital work fighting on the pitch?

The problems stem from the fact that, during the breeding season, certain predatory birds may have to be culled to protect the favoured young grouse. Crows and jackdaws have always been aplenty and culling them to protect the grouse chicks has rarely been a contentious issue. However, falling numbers of raptors, such as the hen harrier, have raised alarm bells and this has called into question the practice of culling known predators of the grouse. This has meant that gamekeepers, part of whose jobs is carrying out such culls, have come to be seen as uncaring monsters, their role in the demise of the hen harrier overshadowing their vital work in caring for the landscape and the wildlife of our uplands.

The true importance of the gamekeeper's role was shown only too graphically when a joint experiment was set up to find out what would happen if predators were left to their own devices. At the start of the experiment that took place on a very famous grouse moor at Langholme in Scotland, the income from the shooting paid for five keepers who tended and managed the heather moorland, controlling the numbers of foxes, stoats and carrion crows. Local hotels and shops benefited from prosperous clients and everyone was happy, including two pairs of hen harriers and a host of other smaller birds that brought birdwatchers into the economic mix.

The keepering was then withdrawn from this area and four years into the experiment the number of hen harriers had soared, with 154 hunting on the wing. Two pairs of peregrine falcons (a species once badly hit by farm chemicals, but now a much more common sight, even nesting on roofs in London) had moved into the area and the very obvious result was that the number of all moorland birds, including our own endemic grouse, had dwindled away.

The official figures gathered by the bird fraternity from the study area and adjacent moors make appalling reading. The reduction in numbers: snipe 51%, curlew 57%, dunlin 80%, golden plover 81%, lapwing 87%, redshank 96%, while in the study area itself, the numbers of meadow pipits and skylarks fell by 80% and ring ouzels by 100%.

Another four years on, the hen harrier numbers were back down to two pairs because there was little left to sustain such a large number of top carnivores, and silent springs, summers and autumns greeted shootists and twitchers alike. The only grouse was from the hotels and shops for, with no income to pay the gamekeepers to control the numbers of predators, there were no grouse to be shot and few birds to be watched.

This one example proves beyond any shadow of doubt that, in a highly-populated country, the conservation of game species for sport does not conflict with the conservation of predators and raptors. Indeed, it is part and parcel of the maintenance of balanced populations of both the hunter and the hunted and all that depends on them. Take away the good gamekeeper and the shootists that pay him and the balance of bird life will change to the detriment of both sportsmen and, of course, birdwatchers.

For vegetarians and vegans there is probably no compromise, but for others please ask yourselves: when it comes to animal welfare, which causes most suffering and which produces the most wholesome food? Grouse flying free-range until "bang" they're dead, or lambs raised on those same fells, before being sent on long, stressful journeys to die in the swill of a slaughterhouse? Sadly, Brussels now demands fewer and bigger slaughterhouses and even condones live export across the Union, exacerbating the latter problem. In the light of all this, surely the perception that killing animals for sport is 'unacceptable' is just hypocrisy, given the general acceptance of mass slaughter of domestic animals for human food.

The way ahead on the moors

The way ahead is surely to continue sustainable management and that will need a lot more understanding and give and take on both sides. In the meantime, we can only dream of the day when all enjoy the spectacle of the sight and sound of the avian food chain from golden plover to golden eagle; all paid for by locally-slaughtered organic spring lamb, autumn grouse and a sustainable supply of well-prepared tourists who can enjoy heather moor honey for tea in visitor centres that enthral, educate and train them, as they drink to the health and safety of the moors.

The central role of grouse shooting in upland management obviously raises the question of access again – walkers' boots and young grouse do not mix. We take it for granted that the general public now have the right to roam over the uplands. It is equally true that the owners of the moorlands should have the right to make a living from their land, so it can remain as most expect it to be.

Is it too much to ask that, during the breeding and the shooting season, the right-to-roamers, especially those with free-range dogs, should go elsewhere? For the rest of the year the moors are there to enjoy, although dogs should be kept on a leash, not only as protection for the wildlife but also for their own protection, since there are already laws that landowners may shoot dogs that are threatening their livelihood. Demands for 24-hour access have sent shivers through the moors (and have prompted important moves for co-operation between landowners and 'land users') but there are worse clouds brooding over our uplands, such as the invasion of trail and quad bikers, who claim the right to roar and all too often cause much damage to the terrain and the peace and quiet. This is another unsustainable BOAT (Byway Open to All Traffic) without a rudder that our bureaucrats have got us into. To cap it all, what about the new website-reported craze of seeing how fast people can drive an internal combustion engine across the tracks of the North York Moors National Park?

Another upland menace is the march of wind turbines across some of the UK's most scenic high areas. This is just one step along the line to the urbanisation of our most visually stunning landscapes. Once the silver satanic windmills are in, complete with grids of service roads and pylons to carry away the intermittent power they generate, will there be anyone left with the will to fight for the rights of those who love our uplands?

There is, hopefully, an answer to this critical question: organisations such as the Heather Trust (see page 68), the Game Conservancy Trust and the Centre for Conservation Science are working in new partnerships with landowners and managers to find the best mix of land management to satisfy all stakeholders. They hope that the application of the results of impartial research, carried out without fear or favour, will be instrumental in resolving conflicts, helping to disperse the 'prejudice, mistrust and hostility' that clouds judgement over this issue.

Best practice across the Pennine Way

One area where you can see examples of how upland management can work is in England's largest and highest National Nature Reserve. This occupies an area of 72 square kilometres around the head-waters of the River Tees in the Northern Pennines. Its outstanding beauty, geology and biodiversity are of international significance, and the site was designated a UNESCO Biosphere Reserve as long ago as 1976. At this time, the site was managed as two separate nature reserves – Moor House, owned by English Nature, and Upper Teesdale, managed by lease from Northumbrian Water and by nature reserve agreement with the Raby and Strathmore farming and shooting estates.

In 1999, the management of the two reserves was integrated into one and, today, a diversity of land use and management practices supports the people and wildlife that live side by side in this unique landscape. Thanks to expert co-operation and sheer hard work, the nationally-threatened black cock is now doing well on the reserve. Upper Teesdale's world-renowned Arctic-Alpine plant communities, relics of the end of the last ice age, survive in their treeless refuge, thanks to better management – although sadly there is evidence of over-grazing. Traditional haymaking continues in the meadows in the dale, providing carpets of flowers, a welcome sight for the people who own the thousands of pairs of feet that trudge through the reserve along the Pennine Way – Britain's most famous long-distance footpath. It's nowhere near perfect yet but what a celebration of diversity, achieved through good communication, integration and mutual respect and support.

Age-old methods of haymaking have helped to maintain the biodiversity of important areas of Upper Teesdale. Many other upland areas have not been so fortunate and over-grazing and the silage revolution have reduced their hill pastures to areas of mat grass, hard rush and thistles of limited value for grazing livestock. Many hill farmers work at the margins of economy and, without supplementary income, they could not make enough money to survive. The foot and mouth outbreak of 2001 brought Britain's hill farming industry to its knees. As if having your entire flock destroyed wasn't bad enough, the closure of vast tracts of land to stop the spread of the disease banished tourists, with devastating consequences for farmers and rural communities.

Catering for the day-trippers

One phoenix that survived the ashes of foot and mouth is Yew Tree Farm, nestling in the heart of the Borrowdale Valley, a jewel of the English Lakes. It is a fine example of the enterprise that is helping to put local food production on the map and is keeping the tourists flocking in! By selling direct to the public and establishing a market for Cumbrian Herdwick lamb and fleeces, Hazel and Joe Relph have turned their 1,600-acre hill farm into a thriving business (see page 63).

Herdwick sheep have grazed the Lakeland fells for hundreds of years, maintaining the balance between heather and grass, and keeping the bracken and scrub at bay. They are a great example of local breeds of hardy animals, stocked at sustainable levels and providing profit while maintaining the biodiversity of the local landscape.

However, we must not underestimate the importance of other forms of tourism in our balanced countryside equation. Contributions from the holiday market sustain the local economy in much of Britain's uplands, thanks to home stays, B&Bs, the YHAs, camping, caravanning and rambling clubs and, more recently, to imaginative schemes such as the British Holiday and Home Parks Conservation Awards and the Lake District Tourism & Conservation Partnership. All this shows that wildlife, people and businesses can exist, not simply side by side, but in working symbiosis.

The University of the Fells

The Lake District, with 23 million day visits and 17 million stay visits in 2002, is already the 'University of the Fells', educating the urban population to understand the ways of the countryside once again. The really good news is that the message of this open-air university is spreading; in 2002, 2.5 million activity holiday trips were made to Scotland by UK residents alone. A Highland visitor survey, carried out between May 2002 and April 2003, interviewed 4,860 people and discovered that, for 67% of them, the opportunity to go on walks was an important part of their visit to the Highlands. 57% of all interviewees also said that wildlife was important to their visit and 31% included bird and wildlife watching in their itinerary.

In fact, the UK Tourist Survey 2001 discovered that watching wildlife is the third most popular outdoor activity amongst UK tourists to Scotland, after walking and golf. As the fortune of Scotland's skiing industry suffers further at the hands of our notoriously intemperate weather and short and long haul competition, income and employment opportunities arising from walking and wildlife holidays assume ever-greater importance in the upland economy. In 1998, visitors on walking holidays to Scotland spent over £438 million. In the same year, skiing accounted for just £15 million of visitor expenditure. In 2001, British tourists alone spent £40 million watching wildlife in Scotland as the main purpose of their trip and this revenue supported around 2,000 jobs. Good access to the countryside and its wildlife is therefore vital to the sustainable health of Scotland's (and in fact the whole of the UK's) rural industry. The implementation of Scotland's Land Reform Act (2003) must, through consultation and participation, balance the needs of the public who wish to enjoy Scotland's countryside, with those of its landowners and occupiers who wish to make a compatible living from it.

Boring as they may seem, the Land Reform (Scotland) Act 2003 and the Countryside and Rights of Way Act 2000 (England and Wales) are two pieces of weighty and lengthy legislation designed to achieve the same goal. As a consequence of the latter, local and national park authorities in England and Wales have been required to set up local access forums that represent landowners, occupiers and other users. Anyone on the way to a meeting of the Stanage Forum will bear witness to the fact that such legislation can and does work. Stacking the odds in favour of two pairs of rare birds breeding in the middle of a rock-climbing motorway is no mean feat; no wonder the conservation world is shouting about it from the heights of the second most-used National Park in the world. And as we are a rich, developed country, we do not have to charge – yet.

As I dot the 'i's' and cross the 't's' of this book, the eyes of scientists from the Natural Environmental Research Council have been turned on our upland grasslands. The bad news is that their studies indicate a marked fall in the number of species of wildflowers growing across our uplands. The cause is put down to the increase of nitrogen in the upland environment allowing the ranker grasses and herbs to grow faster, squeezing out the smaller plants like harebells and eyebright. This is really bad news for the butterflies and other insects that feed on and from them. The causes of this rise in nitrogen could be overstocking of sheep and cattle and the nitrogen oxides released from the tail-pipes of internal combustion engines. Some people point to moor burn as a source of this enrichment, but studies at the Moorhouse Research Station back in the 1960s made much of the fact that burning only recycles the nitrogen that was there already and there was actually a small annual loss. Like the nitrogen, the arguments go round and round but the fact is our uplands need all the care and attention they deserve.

ACCESS

Fact or friction?

Ever since the historic mass trespass on Kinder Scout in 1932, which did more than any other demonstration to secure public access to our open spaces, the issue of access in the British countryside has been a stormy one. Landowners and ramblers have often been at loggerheads about who should be allowed where and exactly what people out and about in the countryside should be allowed to do and when.

The audacity of farmers closing ancient rights of way will always spur the ramblers into action, but the chain reaction causes other crossfire. 'Ramblers have rights': well, if ramblers have rights, so too – say their proponents – do horses and bikes, quad bikes, off-road four-wheelers and landing hot-air balloons. Or do they? Surely common sense tells us that lines must be drawn and the users must be willing to moderate their activities and pay for any damage they cause. Unfortunately, this is all too often not the case.

The good news is that over the years there have been a number of important developments that have helped landowners, ramblers and other people who use the countryside to work together so that a minimum of damage is done. In 1996, for example, the Hillphone service was put in place. This system allows walkers to call a number to find out when and where deerstalking is taking place, so that they can avoid these areas and reduce any disruption to this important part of the rural economy.

However, now the potential impact of access on the environment, and on the livelihoods of the people who work the countryside, has become an even more relevant and pressing issue. New land reform legislation that establishes new statutory rights of public access to the outdoors has recently been passed in Scotland.

The same is happening in England and Wales, where a legal freedom to roam has been introduced under the new Countryside and Rights of Way Act (CRoW); an acronym that is perhaps tainted by the fact that crows are among the real baddies when it comes to countryside management (so please make sure you all know the difference between a crow and a rook, for the latter are OK). As I proof-read the manuscript, some gates are already open and the ramblers are beginning to enjoy their hard-won freedom. The countryside waits to see what the repercussions of these freedoms will be.

The good news is, however, that the crows and the rooks are talking to each other. Rather than wait for problems to occur, many of the concerned parties in Scotland have been brought together to help shape a code of responsibility for good environmentally-sensitive behaviour; a necessary and vital balance if the new rights of access are to become anything more than yet another battleground.

The Scottish Outdoor Access Code was drawn up by Scottish Natural Heritage (SNH) and developed closely with the National Access Forum, an independent group of the main recreational, land managing and public sector organisations with an interest in access. Once it had been drafted, the code was put out to consultation in 2003. Over 1,300 organisations and individuals responded: everyone from individual hill walkers and climbers, through to the big environmental and rambling groups, as well as land managers and landowners. Finding consensus among the responses was a mammoth task, for many were pushing their own single issue points of view; as with the case of single malt whisky buffs, many are loath to budge once they have chosen their preference.

Robust dialogue became the only way ahead, for the players vehemently disagreed on many issues. For example, according to SNH, many farmers argued that in enclosed farmland there should be a physical separation of people from livestock and crops. Not surprisingly, recreational interests countered that access rights do extend to enclosed farmland, except land in which crops have been sown or are growing. In the light of all the comments received, the Code was amended again and again. In the case of public access through fields with livestock, the Code now spells out the possible hazards and risks more clearly and gives more advice on the action people might need to take (including looking for an alternative route) before entering such a field.

It is a complex document and many practical issues will probably take some arguing when push comes to shove. For example, personally I am somewhat lost as to whether deer, grouse, capercaillie and salmon, all of which are managed, come under the definition of a crop. They are certainly of immense importance to the economy of the highlands and islands!

The new Code is based on three key principles and these apply equally to the public and to land managers: respect for the interests of other people, care for the environment and the need for individuals to take responsibility for their own actions. It sets out in detail how people should behave in the countryside, both to each other and to the landscape through which they pass or in which they work.

Despite the need for some compromise, it has been given a cautious welcome by landowners and recreational groups alike. Now the important job is getting the message across. Scottish Natural Heritage has an educational programme to help people understand their responsibilities; it will be interesting to see how they respond. However, through this process a big step has already been taken to ensure that the needs and aspirations of as many people as possible have been taken into account, which will prove vital if our countryside is to be enjoyed by all who wish to do so.

For further information, please see the website at:
www.snh.org.uk/soac

THE STANAGE FORUM

"A strange thing happened to me on the way to the Stanage Forum. I saw a ring ouzel!"

In the summer of 2003, two pairs of ring ouzel, the rare mountain blackbird, successfully nested on Stanage Edge. This is good news, as Stanage Edge lies at the southern limit of the breeding range of this bird in Great Britain and it is reassuring that the area is still a safe outpost for this rare bird.

Stanage Edge is also well-used by climbers. In fact, about 300,000 of them clamber about the rocky outcrop of the Edge each year, making it one of the most popular climbing areas in Britain. That the ring ouzels chose to nest in this rock-climbing hot spot is remarkable. That they successfully raised chicks is astonishing, and that this was achieved with the full support and goodwill of the climbers and other users of the Edge (hang-gliders and paragliders included), who avoided the nest sites, thus depriving themselves of opportunities to pit themselves against all the Edge's physical challenges, is absolutely fantastic!

Stanage Edge, part of the North Lees Estate, lies in the Peak District National Park. The Stanage Forum, set up in August 2000 to help establish a co-operative approach to managing the area, has made a vital contribution to the ring ouzel's breeding success. As the North Lees Estate Manager, Matthew Croney, explained "The key to success was to move forward carefully by voluntary agreement. No-one wants to see protection measures enforced. It's just not the way we work. We follow a participatory approach to managing the estate through the Stanage Forum. As the breeding success of the ring ouzels in 2003 shows, it is really starting to bear fruit. By working together, all parties have been able to improve their understanding of what ring ouzels and people want from the area, and to target ways of helping these rare birds. And, as a lot of people have said, if it can work at Stanage, it can work anywhere!"

By consensus, a series of measures was adopted. Habitat management was undertaken and people were asked to keep their dogs on leads and to avoid certain paths through potential nesting and feeding areas. The Peak District National Park Authority and English Nature provided temporary signs and the birds were carefully monitored throughout the season by the RSPB, volunteer birdwatchers and Estate Wardens. Once the birds had established a nest, people were kept informed as to what was going on through signs, leaflets, website updates and newsletters. All signs carefully explained how and why people could help. Temporary signs were kept to a minimum, were only located close to nest sites where visitor pressure was heaviest, and were removed as soon as the chicks were fledged.

Following the observations made at Stanage Edge during the 2003 ring ouzel breeding season, an unprecedented level of agreement was reached to help the birds again in 2004. The British Mountaineering Council, RSPB, National Park Authority, English Nature, hang-gliders and paragliders agreed to help the ring ouzel's nesting attempts again, and to support measures to avoid key nesting areas in April, when the birds look to establish their nests.

The ring ouzel's breeding success focuses attention on the achievements of the Stanage Forum. "It's great to be working so closely in partnership now," said Matthew. "It just shows what can be achieved through open dialogue."

For further information, please see the Stanage Forum website at:
www.peakdistrict.org/stanage/stanage.htm

YEW TREE FARM

Herdwick sheep keep the tourists flocking in!

Yew Tree Farm is a working, Cumbrian hill farm, whose 1,600 scenically-splendid acres stretch from the grassy pastures around Rosthwaite, a village nestling at the bottom of the Borrowdale Valley, almost to the base of Scafell Pike, England's highest mountain. In common with many farms in the area, Yew Tree Farm is owned by the National Trust, and for many years its tenant farmers, Joe and Hazel Relph, have offered bed and breakfast accommodation to supplement the income they receive from the 2,000 Herdwick sheep they graze on the fells.

Nine years ago, Joe and Hazel opened the Flock In – a tea-room which they created from a converted outbuilding. Lying on both the Cumbria Way and the Coast to Coast Walk, the tea-room proved very popular with long-distance footpath walkers and also with the thousands of other visitors who come to enjoy the area each year. "About 80% of our customers are on a return visit," explains Hazel, emphasising that what's on offer at the Flock In must certainly be worth coming back for.

But the tea-room hasn't only established itself as an excellent watering hole for hungry and thirsty tourists. Joe and Hazel's vision for the Flock In has also allowed them to accomplish something truly remarkable – the establishment of a market for their home-grown Herdwick meat. This market is now so large that, with the help of the National Trust and a grant from Leader Plus, Joe and Hazel are now able to butcher and sell Herdwick meat from neighbouring farms, as well as their own, to meet the ever-increasing demand for this quality product.

The meat is vacuum-packed and sold directly from the tea-room, or it is delivered far and wide by mail order (wrapped in fully biodegradable packaging and kept cool with felt made by a local company from Borrowdale Herdwick fleeces). It also has a starring role on the menu! Not content with selling home-made produce in the tea-room, the Flock In can also boast that much of theirs is home-grown, with their own Herdwick meat the prime ingredient in stews, savoury pastries, pâtés and the Flock In's exclusive 'Herdiburgers'.

What Joe and Hazel are most proud of is the complete traceability of their meat. "The lambs are born here, walk the fells here, get fat here, and within a day of visiting a local abattoir for slaughter, their meat is hung and butchered here to order. Some of the meat is cooked here in the Flock In kitchen and then it is served and eaten here, and the rest is sold here or is sent out from here by mail order."

In 2002, only three years after they began selling their meat direct to the public (one year of which was blighted by the foot and mouth epidemic), Joe and Hazel's achievements were so widely appreciated that they won Radio Four's 'Farming Today' award for the innovative way in which they had forged new links with customers directly, thus cutting out the middle-people in the food production chain. Their farm continues to thrive, with prices for Herdwick lamb from farms in the Borrowdale Valley guaranteed. By selling their Herdwick meat directly to their customers, Joe and Hazel have achieved their goal – to ensure that the traditional farming of Herdwick sheep on the Lakeland Fells remains profitable. "The Farm comes first," says Hazel. "This is just another way of making it viable."

For further information, please see the website at:
www.borrowdaleherdwick.co.uk

Cairn Luchan looking towards Perth, December 1862 – Richard Principal Leitch (c.1827–82)

"The countryside ... is an escape valve, used by a growing number of us to help relieve the pressures of modern life" (page 16)

Among the South Downs – Friedrich Wilhelm Keyl (1823–71)

"Vast areas of woodland ... were cleared for sheep pasture" (page 36)

Manchester from Kersal Moor – William Wyld (1806–70)

"Industrial pollution took its toll on the countryside" (page 42)

View near the west boundary of the Balmoral and Invercauld Forest – James William Giles (1801–70)

"The proper control of the number of deer of all sorts is a vexed question" (page 79)

Sir Walter Scott's favourite view of the Valley of the Tweed, 1887
Tom Scott (1854–1927)

The River Tweed "the most productive salmon river in the North Atlantic system" (page 122)

View over the North Sands (Scarborough) – Henry Barlow Carter (1795–1867)

"Britain is now on its way to having some of the cleanest beaches and bathing waters in Europe" (page 144)

A big shoot at Sandringham – Thomas Jones Barker (1815–82)

"...hunting and shooting have helped shape the British countryside over the past 200 years" (page 169)

Portrait of Billy Duff
Charles Landseer (1799–1879)

"There is still a noble band of around 5,500 gamekeepers hard at work"
(page 170)

SAVING THE BLACK GROUSE

Black grouse display the need for partnership

When it comes to wildlife spectacles, the breeding display of the black grouse must rank as one of the 'best of British'. The arenas in which the showy black cocks (as the males are known) strut their stuff in front of potential mates are called 'leks'. There, the dowdy grey hens (the females) select their ideal partner, mate and then leave the lek to build a nest and lay their eggs without any further involvement from the satisfied male.

The posturing, jumping and calling of the black cocks gathered at a lek, all designed to grab the attention of the visiting females, was once a common sight and sound throughout Britain's upland and lowland heaths. Today 50 years of habitat change – brought about by government policies, grants and subsidies that have encouraged intensive agriculture and large-scale forestry plantations – have caused the local extinction of the black grouse in many regions of Britain. Another problem is predation by foxes, especially on the one-parent families.

Black grouse depend upon the mosaic of habitats that is found where moorland and heath meet woodland, wet scrub and farmland, because here they find the stands of bilberry, heather and cotton grass that provide them with food, shelter and nest sites. Intensive agriculture and large-scale forestry plantation have transformed these mixed habitats that allow the black grouse to thrive into uniform landscapes in which these birds cannot survive.

Between 1988 and 1991, the distribution of black grouse in the UK contracted by 28%. There is evidence that numbers were falling by 10% each year throughout the 1990s – from 25,000 lekking males in 1990 to only 6,510 in 1996, making the black grouse one of the most rapidly declining species in the UK, and one of only 26 bird species for which a UK Biodiversity Action Plan has been produced.*

In an attempt to safeguard this iconic species and its habitat, more than 30 organisations are working in partnership to develop schemes that will retain and recreate the habitat they need. The recommendations for habitat improvement are based on sound scientific research carried out by the Game Conservancy Trust and the RSPB. Landowners, keepers, farmers and foresters are not only informed about what they can do to help, but they are also helped to obtain grants to speed the recommended changes.

It would appear that the efforts of the four national recovery plans targeting remaining populations in Argyll and Bute, Dumfries and Galloway, the North Pennines and Wales are bearing feathered fruit. There have been increases in the numbers of black cock reported in areas of England and Wales where good gamekeeping is practised, animal grazing has been restricted and environmental schemes have been initiated.

Star quality would seem to have been a major incentive in the kick-starting of efforts to save the black grouse from extinction in the UK. They are great crowd pullers, especially at the lek, and with good hides and crowd control no harm need be done. Their crowd-pulling capacity will also help to secure their role as a new tourist attraction for the future, contributing to the local economy.

However, for the ultra-purists the enduring legacy will be the partnerships that have been formed to work towards securing a future for the black grouse and its habitat; a habitat that is also home to hundreds of less charismatic species that may not be as noisy and as glamorous, but are of equal importance to the local balance of nature.

---

* To show you just how many organisations are involved in helping to ensure the future welfare of this bird, take a look at the list below. All

the organisations listed are involved in the England, Scotland and Wales BAP steering groups:

British Association for Shooting and Conservation (Wales), Country Landowners and Business Association (England), Countryside Council for Wales, Deer Commission for Scotland, Department for the Environment, Food and Rural Affairs (England), Durham Biodiversity Partnership (England), English Nature, Farmers Union of Wales, Forestry and Timber Association (Scotland), Forestry Commission England, Forestry Commission Scotland, Forestry Commission Wales, Game Conservancy Trust (England, Wales, Scotland and UK Lead Partner), Heather Trust (Wales), Ministry of Defence (England), Moorland Association (England), National Gamekeepers Organisation (England), National Assembly for Wales Agriculture Department, National Farmers Union of Scotland, National Trust (Wales), NFU Cymru, Northumberland National Park Authority (England), Northumbrian Water (England), Royal Society for the Protection of Birds (England, Wales, Scotland and UK Lead Partner), Scottish Executive Environment and Rural Affairs Division, Scottish Landowners Federation, Scottish Natural Heritage (Scotland and UK Government Contact Point), Severn Trent Water (England), Snowdonia National Park Authority (Wales), Tilhill/EFG Wales, Yorkshire Dales National Park Authority (England).

For further information, please see the BAP website at:
www.ukbap.org.uk

THE HEATHER TRUST

Balancing the moorland equation

The only people who shouldn't trust heather are those allergic to its pollen, for a well-managed heather moorland holds the world record for pollen production. The Heather Trust, an independent Scottish charity, was established in 1994 to encourage a greater understanding of the management of heather moorland through the promotion of best practice. As 25% of Britain's heather moors have been lost since the 1940s, mainly covered by conifers and other crops, careful management of the remainder will be crucial to the survival of this beautiful, man-made, man-managed and (now) almost exclusively British habitat type.

"Management is required to maintain moorland in good condition and a balance between farming, sporting, conservation, recreation and other uses must be established. This balance has been lost in many areas and if it is not regained the diverse range of animal and plant species that we associate with moorland will not survive," Simon Thorp, the Director of the Heather Trust, warns.

To maintain this balance, the Heather Trust promotes four principles of good moorland management:

1. Appropriate vegetation management and heather burning.
2. The management of grazing pressure.
3. Positive, legal vermin control.
4. Management of grouse populations by shooting.

The Heather Trust is one of 22 Scottish conservation and landowning groups that form Scotland's Moorland Forum, a body established by Scottish Natural Heritage in 2002 to seek a sustainable future for Scotland's moors.

However, the Heather Trust also operates across the whole of the United Kingdom and has been awarded a contract by DEFRA to set up four demonstration moorland sites in England and Wales, where best practice can be displayed to all those with and without a vested interest. The sites, in Devon, North Wales, Cumbria and Yorkshire, allow the trust the opportunity not only to develop and share good management practice, but also to make contact with the wide range of people who have a part to play in the maintenance of the moorland landscape, be they land managers such as landowners, farmers, conservationists or gamekeepers, or land users such as walkers or grouse-shooters.

As a member of Scotland's Moorland Forum, the Heather Trust helped to established dialogue between the disparate groups that have a role to play in the balanced management of Scotland's moorland habitats. Simon Thorp is clear about the value of open dialogue to the future health of Britain's moorlands. "In the modern era, the partnership approach is vital if progress is to be achieved and the condition of our moorland areas improved. It can be surprising how much groups that appear to hold opposing views can have in common."

For further information, please see the website at:
www.heathertrust.co.uk

PATHWAYS TO PARTNERSHIP

Adding a little on the bill for conservation

Castlerigg Hall Caravan and Camping Park lies in a quiet, elevated position, three kilometres from the centre of Keswick, with magnificent views of Derwent Water, Bassenthwaite Lake and the surrounding fells. During the autumn of 2002, the Park became a member of the Lake District Tourism & Conservation Partnership (see page 73 for more details). They started to involve visitors to the park in local practical conservation projects; in their case, the repair of badly-eroded local footpaths through a visitor payback scheme. The Castlerigg scheme gives visitors the chance to make a voluntary contribution of £2.00 to the scheme when they make a reservation. For every £1.00 raised, the Heritage Lottery Fund matches it with a further £2.00.

"We are delighted to have the opportunity to help raise funding towards these footpath repair projects, only two miles from our Park," says David Jackson, whose family have farmed Castlerigg Hall since 1938 and began to develop it as a camping and caravan park in the 1950s.

At the end of January 2004, visitors to Castlerigg Hall had voluntarily contributed £1,055.00 to the footpath repair appeal, which aims to raise £2,500.00 towards the repair of footpaths on nearby Bleaberry Fell and Walla Crag – areas enjoyed by many of the Park's visitors. The work on Bleaberry Fell – where there is a 300 metre-long erosion scar – is particularly important since this is part of a sensitive heather habitat of European significance that has been identified by the National Park Authority and the National Trust as needing urgent attention.

For David, participation in the Lake District Tourism & Conservation Partnership has brought a new dimension to Castlerigg's conservation work. "We felt as a tourism operator it was important to try and put something directly back into the local area, particularly as it was partly visitor pressure that was creating some of the problems of erosion. Beforehand, other than local litter picks and helping local sports groups and charities through sponsorship, conservation work was primarily done on the park itself. But by joining this group we were able to raise funds through a visitor payback scheme to help with repair work to fell paths that had become badly eroded. This has proved very popular, with over 90% of guests who pre-book making a contribution."

The decision to join the partnership represented another conservation milestone for Castlerigg, already a four-times Gold Award Winner in the David Bellamy Conservation Award Scheme for its implementation of measures that allow the site to be enjoyed equally by people and wildlife.

The site's owner, David Jackson, is very positive about the benefits that participation in the Conservation Award Scheme has brought. "Without the encouragement from the British Holiday and Home Parks Scheme, and seeing the benefits that have followed, I doubt whether we would have participated in other schemes. I feel some conservation schemes are just a PR exercise, without any real commitment to the environment, whereas the Bellamy scheme actively encourages work to be carried out 'on the ground' rather than a paper policy with little or no substance."

An example of this type of work at Castlerigg was the delivery of a consignment of buddleia plants, designed to provide a food source for the many species of butterfly. "I was amazed at the number of butterflies that were on just five of these plants during the summer; I counted 21 one morning," says David. "The accompanying information board ensured that the customers understood what we were trying to achieve. We followed this by taking over 100 cuttings from the original plants for the following season. Members of our staff were equally enthusiastic, taking cuttings for their own gardens; even the bank manager ended up taking four plants home when he visited!"

For David, another good example of practical action was the Bellamy Conservation Day at Skelwith Fold Caravan Site, Ambleside. "One of the guest speakers was an owl expert from Muncaster Castle who explained the habitat required for owls. Although we once had an owl at Castlerigg we hadn't heard or seen it for a few years, but once we implemented the advice about leaving areas of grass uncut, which would allow fieldmice to flourish thus providing a food source, an owl returned."

Overall, Castlerigg shows what can be done by a local business to help solve local environmental problems.

For further information, please see the website at:
www.castlerigg.co.uk

THE LAKE DISTRICT TOURISM & CONSERVATION PARTNERSHIP

The business of conservation

If you've ever sweated your way up to the top of a mountain in the Lake District, spare a thought for the people who help maintain the paths you walk on; people like Pete Entwhistle who has recently completed work on Harrison Combe in the Langdale Pikes. The work takes dedication – the path laying and erosion control necessary to keep the landscape intact is hard graft! Luckily, Pete's team is supported by a local tourism company who have raised over £73,400 for the work.

"Every year many thousands of visitors enjoy the splendour of the English Lake District. The ravages of nature, the Lakeland weather and the pounding of countless boots and bikes all take their toll on this unique environment," explains Kirstie Royce, Director of the Lake District Tourism & Conservation Partnership. "That's why footpath work is so important." To support this vital effort, the Partnership run the 'Our Man at the Top' scheme, which has helped get support for three teams of path restorers, including Pete's. Overall, the 170 businesses involved in the scheme have raised over £138,800 for footpath work in various parts of the Lakes.

As its name suggests, the Partnership brings together tourism companies that want to help the environment with the people who are involved in practical projects 'on the ground'. Established in 1993, growing membership has raised significant amounts of money for all sorts of vital conservation projects. "As we hit the late 90s we saw a big increase in business support," says Kirstie. "The main thing that local business people get out of it is that it provides a great way of engaging with their visitors – next time they come to the hotel or caravan park they ask, 'How is my path going?'"

This means that the scheme allows local businesses to work with their customers in a whole new way. Many of these businesses are long-established and, as Kirstie notes, helping them to conserve Lakeland also offers them an opportunity to "put something back". To do this, many businesses in the Lakes now operate visitor payback schemes and voluntary levies, which benefit footpath repair, bridge restoration, habitat protection, woodland management and so much more. "We tipped the £½ million mark in 2003," says Kirstie, highlighting the level of business support the scheme now receives.

A decade of stunningly successful partnership was marked by a project with the National Trust to raise money to conserve Birdhouse Meadows, one of the most important wet meadow habitats in the Lake District. "The meadowland habitat will be carefully managed to allow a variety of birds, bats, frogs, toads, wildflowers and grasses, butterflies and dragonflies to thrive!" enthuses Kirstie. "The boardwalk route around the site, which takes walkers over marshy areas, will also be improved, as will the existing footpath." In this way, the partnership hopes that, with the help of hotels and other tourist companies, nature will benefit and so will the visitors who want to see it – the result: happy wildlife, happy tourists and happy hoteliers.

Personally, I am astounded by the success of Kirstie and her team: what an organisation the LDTCP has become! Nowhere else I know are visitor payback schemes so focused and so successful. The voluntary schemes have a staggering 99% uptake rate with visitors, and have been embraced by the tourism industry. But then I would be enthusiastic, wouldn't I, since they made me their President!

For further information, please see the Partnership website at:
www.lakespartnership.org.uk

Chapter 4

FORESTS WITH A FUTURE

At Pound Farm in Suffolk, a new wood is growing. Until 1989 the 223-acre site was an arable farm with only about 11 acres of existing woodland. Since then over 70,000 trees have been planted and 160 acres of woodland created. Taking a walk through the site is to see a wonderful transformation taking place. Surrounded by a deer fence to protect the young trees, the new wood boasts grassy rides, meadowland, streams and ponds amongst its new stands of oak, ash, hornbeam and other native trees characteristic of the heavier Suffolk soils on which it grows.

The importance of Pound Farm lies not just in the diversity of habitats it contains, or in the variety of plants and animals that already make it their home, but in the fact that new woods like it hold part of the key to re-establishing the balance of nature across the British countryside.

Pound Farm is a great example of many new forests bèing grown by one of Britain's most upstanding conservation groups, the Woodland Trust. The Trust, working with local people, already cares for around 19,000 hectares (47,000 acres) of woodland across the length and breadth of Britain. They have recently created 200 new woods in England and Wales and 50 more in Northern Ireland to celebrate the Millennium (see page 98). Their vision puts the protection, restoration and creation of woodland squarely – although its blocks of trees are anything but square – at the heart of nature conservation in Britain. "Woodland has the potential to refresh the appearance of the countryside [I would add the words 'adding majesty'], creating genuine opportunities for wildlife to regain a foothold and set right the fragmentation of our wild places over the last century," the Trust says. This is a great example of the joined-up thinking that is putting balance back into our countryside.

Forests for life

The Trust is not alone in its belief that woodland is a vital ingredient in the restoration of balance in the British countryside. People love trees and there is no getting away from the fact that when they are planted or re-planted in the correct mix, in the right places, they add to the landscape immeasurably and provide invaluable habitats for animals and plants to thrive and places for people to enjoy.

As organisations such as Common Ground have long realised, woodland and orchards give much of rural Britain its living character and brings many benefits, not only to the wildlife that live inside it but also to the human communities that live nearby. In fact, it has been scientifically shown that walking in a wood is good for our health and that a hospital bed overlooking green space and woodland speeds the healing process. Add to this the fact that woods and forests clean the air of pollution and recycle carbon dioxide as they grow, while breathing out water vapour and oxygen. It's no wonder that woodland is environmental good-guy number one.

Unfortunately, despite the work of groups like the Woodland Trust, Britain still has a long way to go before the full potential of native trees to revitalise the British countryside is fully realised.

People have been knocking Britain's ancient woods about ever since Neolithic axemen started polishing their greenstone choppers. However, it was not until the close of the First World War that Britain's woodlands came to a post-ice age all-time low when only 5% of these islands was covered with trees, most of them being important parts of hunting and shooting estates. Something had to be done and David Lloyd George helped dream up the Forestry Commission. This was set up not only to grow pit props should another war cut off our post-empire-ical supply, but also to provide more people with free access to the country.

In the second half of the twentieth century 'economic forestry' became the watchword and the world watched as a great diversity of habitats, often in the UK's wildest places, were ploughed and planted thanks to government subsidises that welcomed alien conifers. One reason, perhaps, that we are not as proud as other nations of our National Forest.

In more recent times, the madness of this policy has given way to a much more wildlife and tourist-friendly mantra of 'sustainable multi-use forestry', welcoming millions of visitors every year to the one million plus hectares now under management by the three National Forest Enterprise Agencies on behalf of the Forestry Commission. My branch is Hamsterley Forest in County Durham and it is a grade one Site of Special Scientific Interest three times over. It's a super place to walk, ride, mountain bike and see a cross-section of Britain's wildlife as you go.

In the most recent Forest Strategy for England, the Commission has been given the target of creating 15,000 hectares of new woodland, not this time to help the coal industry but to prop up the rural economy through nature-based tourism and arboriculture. Proper wildlife management is also high on the new forestry agenda: for example, deer fences that can kill capercaillie and other birds are now being replaced by selective culling carried out by highly-dedicated forest rangers. Sale of stalking rights and of venison adds to the forest revenue. Add to this the Ancient Woodland Project being run by Forest Enterprise, which aims to return plantations on ancient woodland sites to stands of native trees, and the future certainly looks a little brighter (see page 95 for more details).

Dreams and targets

It's easy to dream dreams and set targets, but recently over 80 ancient woodlands – the holy grail of conservation – have been damaged by road building work and some 300 others are currently under threat.

Of those that do remain, many are not properly managed or do not have the best mix of trees to encourage wildlife and discourage invaders like grey squirrel, muntjac and sika – who are not the little dears some think them to be. But most disturbing is the fact that Britain remains one of the least-wooded countries in Europe. In fact, trees only cover about 11.5% of Great Britain, against a European average of about 30%. Most damaging from a wildlife point of view is the fact that only 1.2% of the UK is cloaked with anything that approaches ancient semi-natural woodland.

Personally, I would like to see at least 25% of the UK once again cloaked in broad-leaf woodland bursting with native biodiversity (we used to call it wildflowers and wildlife), providing a place for us all to go and de-stress as we 'walk with the trees'. I would like to see these woodlands buffering the effects of plantations and, when near centres of population, augmented by short-term rotation coppices stripping polluting nutrients from the soil while providing biodiverse habitats and local supplies of fuel.

The Woodland Trust threw the government a similar challenge for the Millennium, suggesting that there should be freely-accessible woodland within ten miles of everyone.

So what can be done? Can Britain's commercial woodlands combine making a profit with looking after the wildflowers and wildlife? How can Britain bring back the diverse and wildlife-rich woods that were once the flagship of our natural heritage?

The truth is that if we just walked away and left nature to its own devices, much of Britain would return to woodland, as it has many times in the past. However, thanks to the impact of a plethora of weeds and feral animals, this would be a long and tortuous process. Obviously the job of re-forestation can be speeded with community action based on good science.

There are also over 200,000 hectares of disturbed 'brownfield' land and much more degraded farmland, a good deal of which would benefit from the therapeutic touch of the right mix of trees planted by us humans in the right places.

Volunteers: a growing band of very important people

The good news is that all across the UK, a varied group of like-minded people – from foresters and farmers, Wildlife Trusts and other groups such as the British Trust for Conservation Volunteers (BTCV) and the Woodcraft Folk, to local governments and urban volunteers are all working to protect, enhance and restore the nation's sylvan heritage.

One example of this pioneering work is that of the Scottish group, Trees for Life. Relying mainly on the work of dedicated volunteers, the group has the grand vision of restoring a large area of the Caledonian Forest that used to cover much of Scotland.

By the end of spring 2000, more than 410,000 Scots pine and native broad-leaf saplings had been planted – demonstrating in no uncertain terms what can be achieved given vision and determination (see page 100 for details). Deer fencing is a major cost for groups like these, but is absolutely necessary because of the breeding success of these voracious browsers.

The proper control of the number of deer of all sorts is a vexed question, and a main source of division, in the countryside debate. However it is a vital process that, as the government now agrees, can best be done by trained stalkers and their paying clients.

Fortunately for the trees, more people are learning the value of organic free-range venison to a healthy diet! Environmentalist Neil

Duncan, working in the mists of the Mull of Kintyre, has even demonstrated how an economic herd of red deer can be harvested sustainably in native broad-leaf forest that was their original habitat. Surely it is the right of every deer to have access to good grazing (even before they become organic venison).

The need for animal control, culling and harvesting obviously brings up the issue of animal rights. Of course animals have rights, but the question, surely, is how should these be prioritised? What about when rats, locusts, mosquitoes, midges and even tigers, lions and elephants come into conflict with human health and best practice in landscape management? With six billion people trying to make a living off this planet, some form of control is necessary. Take away deer and rabbit control and the farmers and foresters would be out of work. Stop controlling foxes and free-range chickens would really become a thing of the past. Stop culling rats and mice and our cities would soon be unliveable. Stop controlling mink and the cry to legally control cormorants and other fish-eating birds that now home in on our fish-farms would be heard even louder.

This is a cross we humans have to bear. Sadly, the killing must go on and, as humans, we must do it in the kindest way possible. In many cases, dogs to find the animals and well-trained guns to shoot them are the order of the way ahead. All I can say is, as long as there are people willing to be paid to do it and others who will pay to be part of this vital management team in the name of sport, the better it is for us who couldn't pull the trigger or clear up the carcasses.

Back to the trees: volunteers and non-government organisations (NGOs) – like Trees for Life – and their teams of skilled helpers are at the heart of many of the most important forest conservation programmes in the UK. From the task-forces of the Woodland Trust and the British Trust for Conservation Volunteers to the nationwide networks of the Wildlife Trusts, the National Trust and the RSPB, tens of thousands of committed individuals are at work protecting, managing and planting trees and, of course, raising money to speed this vital work.

Volunteers are also a key part of one of the boldest long-term conservation projects in the UK – the development of the National Forest and the 12 Community Forests (see page 103 for details on these). Started on a cold winter's day in 1990, the National Forest is a project aimed to improve forest cover over 200 square miles of the Midlands. The Forest's boundary takes in parts of the counties of Derbyshire, Leicestershire and Staffordshire, an area which could then only boast about 6% woodland cover (much less than the national average). It encompasses a number of towns and villages, miles of rolling farmland and a former coalfield which was in desperate need of regeneration.

Since the start in March 2002, about five million trees have been planted, more than doubling woodland cover in the Forest area and moving the project well on its way to its target of 30 million new trees. That will bring woodland cover in the area up to around 30%, benefiting wildlife, local residents and businesses and attracting more visitors.

The National Forest, like the majority of forest creation schemes, depends on creating partnerships between landowners, farmers, local authorities, companies, local communities and NGOs. This has meant that getting the resources and incentives to pull together the wide range of groups needed for the Forest's successful creation and future management has been really hard work; not as much fun as planting the tress themselves but just as important.

Getting money for planting trees could be a bit easier in the future, especially for farmers. Recent reforms in the Common Agricultural Policy look set to make more money available for farmers to grow trees and woodlands. These 'agri-environment' schemes are already achieving great things. For example, according to

DEFRA, ancient, dying woodland in Dentdale, Cumbria, is being restored by work funded under the Pennine Dales Environmentally Sensitive Areas scheme.

However, grants are finite and can only go so far. So what can be done to make up the difference?

Using the market to save the trees

In recent years, many environmentalists and foresters have also been looking to the market to boost the biodiversity of Britain's forests and add to their acreage. It's a tough call, especially since timber prices are low at the moment; however, if the economics of woodlands are really looked into, it starts to make common sense.

A recent survey underlined just how important woodlands can be to the nation's purse when it revealed that the woods and forests in the south west of England are worth an amazing £575 million to the region's economy, providing over 16,000 jobs. The report looked at the value of the timber industry but also the wider uses of woodland, such as tourism and education and even at the effect that forests have on our health and that of the balance of the water catchment they affect.

One of the most important initiatives now under way across the UK, to turn the economic potential of woods into new and better-managed woodland, is forestry certification; in other words, giving timber and other woodland products that have been grown and harvested in an environmentally-friendly way a 'stamp of approval'. A stamp that lets the consumer (whether its someone buying paper or a builder buying timber) know that they are helping to improve the UK's habitat.

The most important label is the UK Woodland Assurance Standard (UKWAS). According to the Forestry Commission, certification under this standard has expanded rapidly in the UK, and there are now over 1.1 million hectares of UKWAS certified forest and woodland – about 40% of the UK's total forest area. The label is linked to the international Forest Stewardship Council's (FSC) certification scheme (see page 89).

It is still relatively early days for the label and it is therefore unclear exactly what impact the standard is having. A recent report for the UKWAS Support Unit found that, generally, there had only been small improvements in how forests were managed after they became certified. This was put down to the fact that most certified forests were already managed with the environment in mind before they joined the scheme.

However, what is clear is that, for the standard to have any real impact, it must be made more widely known so that demand for certified products increases, creating an impetus for woodlands that are currently poorly-managed to be brought up to standard, benefiting both the animals and plants that live in them and the families that live off them.

One example of what can be achieved is the work of the BioRegional Charcoal Company. Set up in 1995, the company works with a network of about 40 independent charcoal burners to supply retailers such as B&Q. The products that the company supply are from well-managed forests that are local to the point of sale. All the products carry the Forest Stewardship Council (FSC) logo. This innovative business allows small-scale producers to make a living managing woodland in the right way. According to the company, products from 68 woodlands encompassing over 4,000 hectares of broad-leaf trees across Britain are currently certified.

Fuel for thought

Charcoal is not the only fuel that can come from woodland; just think about what you normally put on your bonfire. The production of energy from wood, mainly willow produced in a process called 'short-rotation' coppicing, is another string in the economic bow of forestry. It has had a bumpy history recently; the most ambitious wood-fired power-station in the country – the ARBRE bio-energy plant in North Yorkshire – went into liquidation. However, the future of this business now looks more secure with wood-fuel producers focusing on smaller-scale power plants such as the 700kW woodchip-fuelled boiler that powers Worcestershire County Hall.

Many other local authorities are looking into the potential of wood-fired boilers to power and heat facilities such as schools and swimming pools and many farmers and forestry companies are investigating the potential market for wood as fuel. For example, a group of farmers in Staffordshire is pioneering the transformation of biomass directly to electricity in small-scale units made by Talbotts, a local heat engineering company.

This may sound like bad news for the environment; however, coppiced woodland is actually a rich habitat that provides many environmental benefits alongside the potential financial returns. Given that up to 40% of existing lowland woodland is currently under-managed and the importance of the revenue from managing woodland as coppice becomes immediately apparent.

Tourism is another economic sector that directly benefits from the conservation of woodlands. In the south west study it was found that the use of woodlands for leisure generated well over £300 million a year and that many businesses such as riding stables, and home, holiday, camping and caravanning parks gained much benefit from it. In the light of this information, it is not surprising that many tourism operators are responding to the public's fondness for woods with working holidays and visitor centres. Woodlands also support many other money-making enterprises, from willow wand production to mountain bike hire shops and from orienteering to paintball wars.

From an historical point of view, country sports are one of the most venerable economic uses of woodland. This is because woods are the most important habitat for quarry and important game-birds during the winter months.

From the days of the royal forests, country sports have been an important reason for woodland conservation, management and creation. Today, many pheasant woods are identified in English Nature's Inventories of Ancient Woodland and some are designated Sites of Special Scientific Interest (SSSIs). Pheasant shooting now provides a big incentive for many private landowners to keep and manage their woodland habitats.

Sylvan services

Of course, the value of forests is not just the profits that can be made from selling the timber and other products. Forests also provide the only habitat for many native plants and animals while carrying out a whole range of vital environmental 'services', from regulating water-tables and stream flow to slowing erosion and storing energy in carbon rich wood, all solar powered.

Until recent times, it was widely appreciated that as trees grow they help regulate the amount of carbon dioxide and oxygen in the atmospheric envelope. However, in the past 20 years the release of carbon dioxide due to the burning of fossil fuels has begun to be blamed for overheating what is now called the global greenhouse, with dire consequences ranging from increased storms, floods and droughts to catastrophic melting of the ice caps and consequent rising of the sea level.

Upheavals in the weather are now in the news every day, with climate scientists proclaiming that the build-up of this gas in the atmosphere is mainly to blame.

We are, however, rarely reminded that clouds are made of water vapour and that if all the water vapour was removed from the atmosphere the temperature would drop by 32 degrees Celsius. In contrast, if all the carbon dioxide was removed from the atmosphere the temperature would only drop by about one degree but photosynthesis, and hence life as we know it, would come to an end.

There is, of course, a complication for, as warm damp air rises, it becomes cooler and some of the water vapour it contains condenses to form droplets or even ice crystals– the stuff clouds are made of. Clouds not only help to trap heat in but also form sun shades, reflecting the incoming radiation from the sun, again helping to keep the natural balance. Anyone who takes a walk in the countryside will tell you that the hottest days and the coldest nights are those without a cloud in the sky.

So there is no getting away from the fact that water vapour is the most abundant greenhouse gas, accounting for 96% of the greenhouse effect. What is more, 99.999% of the water vapour is there thanks to Mother Nature.

Meanwhile, the climate scientists who blame global warming on rising levels of atmospheric carbon dioxide do their best to ignore the complex role of water vapour as the natural damp blanket that traps the infra-red radiation as it beams in and so helps to keep the temperature of our planet on regulo 'life'. Yet even with the rise in carbon dioxide concentration, at which the global warmers wag their computers, there is evidence that forests across the world are already in on the balancing act, soaking at least some of it up. One can only wonder how much carbonated Perrier was carted around the world to cool all the hot air that became part of the Kyoto protocol.

Of course, it is being argued that even a tiny rise in temperature caused by carbon dioxide could trigger all this disruptive weather and worse that is costing people and their insurance companies much more than a lot of worry. Acts of Mother Nature or acts of infernal combustion engines? Well, that is for the litigation lawyers to decide.

Meanwhile back to forests; if carbon induced global warming is true then a key part of the fight against climatic disruption could be the saving of forests and the planting and proper management of the right trees in the right places. Fortunately, this is as true for trees in the UK as for those of the Amazon. Even if it isn't true, and there are a lot of scientists who do not believe in carbon dioxide-induced global warming, trees, woodlands and forests play so many other important roles that the same implies that trees have an important part to play in all our futures.

The importance of trees is highlighted by the work being done by the city of Newcastle-upon-Tyne, which has set itself the goal of becoming 'carbon-neutral'; in other words it will, on balance, not produce any carbon dioxide.

The city where investors were once warned 'not to carry coals to' is working to create long-term, well-managed woodlands mainly made up of native species. One strange twist in this tale is that their chosen mascot is Daisy the Cow. Perhaps she was genetically modified to produce no methane, for that is a much more potent greenhouse gas than carbon dioxide!

Right or wrong, the battle to stop global warming may be the magic ingredient that will really kick-start a woodland renaissance in the UK. Wood-fired power plants are already in line for funding from the 'renewables obligation' that requires all electricity suppliers to get a percentage of their power from renewable sources.

This in itself is a very important idea because the world is rapidly using up all the fossil fuels, which are non-renewable. So paying people to plant renewable stocks of local energy in the form of wood, even if the excuse is just to soak up carbon dioxide, is a sensible thing to do. If only they would pay people to leave the rest of the ancient woodlands left on earth standing, we would really be getting somewhere.

It must also be pointed out that a wood fire is but an incinerator in disguise and that crematoria that often intrude into the green belt are, along with Bonfire Night, one of the major spot sources of dioxins in Britain. Real facts about the pros and cons of incineration are needed as small-scale local supplies of alternative energy come on-stream to help solve the problems of energy supply and rural economics.

The future for forestry

So what does the future hold for forestry in the UK? Given the positive initiatives currently under way, it is to be hoped that more and more landowners will join forces with environmentalists to put back more of the UK's lost woodland heritage. The dream is for a much more wooded Britain, with well-managed, ecologically-diverse native woodlands in the right places supplying vital environmental services, while providing a sustainable livelihood for many rural communities.

The large forests and woods of Britain – old and new alike – will obviously be the centre-pieces of sylvan Britain, joined by well-managed hedgerows and other 'green corridors' such as canals, riparian forests, rural roads and woodlands in the right places alongside motorways and railways: corridors of shade, themselves acting as migration routes complete with service stations and overnight accommodation, all in place to service wildlife migrating in either direction depending on the vagaries of climatic change.

To bring all this to fruition will require everyone to realise the importance of woodlands and the ways in which they can help – whether by buying the 'right' woodland products, by contributing to woodland conservation as tourists, by giving money to woodland charities or by rolling up their sleeves and joining in the planting and ongoing management themselves.

TALKING OF TREES

The Duchy of Cornwall and the FSC

Just like another famous plant person, I have always thought there is nothing odd about talking to trees. His Royal Highness the Prince of Wales' passion for all things horticultural doesn't just stop in the garden, it extends to the hundreds of hectares of woodland that are part of the Duchy of Cornwall.

The extent of the Prince's passion for woodland conservation is shown by the fact that his estates contain private woods which were among the first in Britain to obtain Forest Stewardship Council (FSC) certification. The move towards this goal started in 1996 and since then almost all of the Duchy's woodlands, in both Cornwall and Herefordshire, have come into the scheme. This means that customers can buy timber products from the Duchy safe in the knowledge that the woodlands in which they grew have added value to this royal seal of approval.

"There is little doubt that we have seen a marked improvement in wildlife as we have established a greater diversity of habitats," says Geraint Richards, the Duchy's Head Forester, who explains that conservation work on the Duchy estates includes everything from removing conifers from the borders of forest rides to making sure that contractors use biodegradable chainsaw oil if possible. "Coppice management and the establishment of natural reserve areas and long-term retention stands is all part of our work," he says, adding that when the Duchy thins hardwoods they leave veteran trees and deadwood to encourage wildlife.

Large old native trees are of great importance, not only adding majesty to the landscape but a continuity of ecological purpose. They are high-rise habitats for, even in the case of a single English oak, they provide homes to hundreds of species of insects and other creepy crawlies: a royal banquet for woodpeckers and the like. What is more, as their life comes to an end, the rotting wood fuels another part of the food chain, nature's own binmen, the decomposers that reduce, reuse and recycle the raw materials on which sustainable forest life depends.

Current key projects in the Duchy's woodlands include the restoration of native habitats in plantation areas. "The Duchy has replaced stands of alien trees such as Western Hemlock with native broad-leaf species," says Geraint, who explains that biodiversity and habitat management such as this is part and parcel of a whole FSC package which includes public access and timber production, with all their challenges of health and safety.

The woodlands managed by the Prince's team are a mixture of ancient semi-natural broad-leaved woodland, plantations on ancient woodland sites and recent plantations that were established on agricultural land. Some areas are important enough in wildlife terms to be designated as Sites of Special Scientific Interest (SSSIs). One such 70-acre SSSI provides a royal home for the rare heath fritillary butterfly and the wood in this region is specifically managed to help the insect thrive.

The drive for certification has been an important factor in the success of the ecological management of the Duchy's woodland. "It has focused the mind," says Geraint. "We have always been environmentally-positive managers of our woodland, but we probably wouldn't have set as significant targets on issues such as plantation restoration and the establishment of reserve areas. It has also pushed us forward on smaller details such as making sure that our contractors use as few and as environmentally-friendly chemicals as possible."

Certification has also been important from a commercial point of view. "Now certification becomes the norm it is vital for people like us to do it, so that we keep our market share," says Geraint, who underlines the fact that, given the poor state of the timber market in Britain today, landowners have to do everything possible to stay competitive.

The need for certification has been particularly significant for paper pulp sales, which make up a large percentage of the market for the Duchy's forest products. The Duchy woods also supply fencing, sawn logs and more specialised and high quality timber for local boat-builders in Cornwall and for craftsmen, joiners and other craft people in Herefordshire.

The work that's being done on the Duchy estates and in other well-managed woodlands across Britain is vital. The truth of the matter is that it is not just the royal prerogative to be at one with nature, we all talk to trees and what is more they all answer back in a very practical way. As we talk, the carbon dioxide we exhale is used by plants to make more plants. These add beauty to the land and provide food for the ravenous hoards of natural reducers, reusers and recyclers that make the living world go round and round and round. What is more, as they do it all green plants make oxygen which we all need and water vapour which is the main greenhouse gas that maintains the global greenhouse on regulo 'life'.

Because plants are so important, we all should do everything we can to support projects that keep Britain's flora, and hence fauna, thriving. Labelling schemes, like the FSC's, give us a great way of doing just that. For example, when you put pen or printer to paper, why not do it in the most environmentally-friendly way, on paper with the hallmark FSC?

For further information, please see the website at: www.fsc.org

REFUGES FOR RED SQUIRRELS

Making space amongst the greys

When I was young, red squirrels were common across the length and breadth of Britain. Sadly, thanks to the invasion of its grey cousin, which was introduced from America, our native squirrel has been driven out from much of its territory. In England red squirrels are now hanging on in only a few isolated pockets of the country, like the Isle of Wight, Cumbria, Northumberland and Merseyside. Today there are only 30,000 left in England, compared with two million of the grey invaders and, although they are still widespread in Scotland, here their numbers are also under attack from the alien greys.

Red squirrels are just one of the many species of plants and animals that used to play an important part in the balance of our native woodlands but have been pushed to the brink of extinction by competition from outsiders, a process that has been accelerated by changes that have taken place in our woodland habitats.

Now, thanks to the hard work and dedication of conservationists around the country, there is a red light at the end of the squirrel drey. A red light that will help stop the advance of the grey invaders and give the red, one of the most endearing of our woodland creatures, a chance of survival. To ensure this survival, groups such as Red Alert North West are busy creating forest reserves for the red squirrels where they are given the habitat they need and where the greys are *persona non grata*.

This type of work – which involves restoring and managing forests so that they can better support native species – shows just how important woodland habitat management is to wildlife conservation in the UK. The reserves have been chosen because they contain a mix of trees in which the invading greys do not appear to thrive. Ironically, these forests are large conifer blocks and, whilst they deter the greys, they favour the reds. The fact that today there seems to be a place for the once much-maligned conifer forest goes to show how we have to be prepared to adopt a flexible and pragmatic approach to conservation challenges.

As I write, Red Alert North West has created two of these red squirrel reserves in Cumbria: one in Thirlmere and a second in Whinfell forest. The latter is in conjunction with the Lowther Estate and Center Parks and already thousands of holidaymakers can enjoy daily encounters with our native 'Squirrel Nutkin'.

Ecologist Jason Reynolds is driving the project forward. He explains that the reserves have also been located in areas where there is not too much surrounding woodland, reducing the likelihood of greys arriving on the scene. "These are already honeypots of reds," he says. "We work with foresters to make sure that the forest has the correct mixture of trees. Trees such as Norway spruce are grown specifically to provide the reds with food and any greys are trapped and humanely killed where necessary. Education and access, through the provision of viewing hides and guided walks, also underpin the message of red squirrel conservation, enthusing others to lend their support."

It's hard work, but very worthwhile. The reserves are the first in a proposed string of 20 across northern England. Groups in Scotland, Wales and Northern Ireland are also due to set up forest reserves too. The areas involved are quite substantial; for example, Whinfell is about the size of 650 football pitches and is currently home to 150 red squirrels. The success of the whole project rests on the support of landowners who, like the Lowther Estate and Center Parks, have an economic stake in the process. As Jason reports, it is only with supportive stakeholders like these on board that conservation can really move into top gear.

Just as important is sponsorship and donations from the public, to fund the work that must be done to give red squirrels a toe-hold from which they might re-establish themselves – a treetop presence showing us that their woodland home is coming back into the right sort of balance.

For further information, please see the website at:
www.redsquirrel.org.uk

PAWS FOR THOUGHT

Putting the 'old' back in our forests

Pause a moment to take in the fact that the Forestry Commission takes care of almost 1,000,000 hectares of land, which supplies us with all manner of forest products from bark chips to paper. It looks after many Sites of Special Scientific Interest (SSSIs), all crucially important areas for their geology, wildflowers and wildlife and most of which are central features in many areas of outstanding natural beauty. No wonder over 50 million visitors made use of this fantastic resource for healthful rest and exercise in 2003.

If you go down in those woods today, you are in for a pleasant surprise – our native wildlife is making a real comeback. Sadly, by the 1960s, much of the UK's ancient woodland areas had been extensively replanted with conifers and some with beech, to the detriment of the wildlife that used to live in them. Now things are changing fast thanks to schemes such as the Ancient Woodland Project, managed by the Forestry Commission.

A glimpse of what the future holds for visitors can be seen at Wharncliffe Wood, which straddles the Sheffield/Barnsley border. Here, in this woodland of almost 450 hectares, conifers are being selectively thinned to make way for trees native to this country.

Some areas will also be left as open space so you can see the woods despite the trees, whilst encouraging heathland, home of many flowers, animals and birds including the fabulous nocturnal nightjar. The sale of timber will help finance the 'back to nature' plan, which will see the wood completely broad-leaf by the year 2045.

A similar move is planned for Old Park and Hugset Woods, also near Barnsley, where the alien conifers are destined for the chop. "This is a major step forward," said Albin Smith, Forester for South Yorkshire.

"Large areas of conifers were planted at Wharncliffe in the 1950s as part of a drive to create a timber reserve following the war. Now priorities have changed and conservation ranks among the Forestry Commission's most important objectives."

According to Albin, the end result will be a mixture of habitats ranging from woodland, heathland and wood pasture to ponds and high quality stands of broad-leaf.

The scheme is just a tiny part of a nationwide push to protect, conserve and expand ancient woodland on Forestry Commission estates and to restore plantations on ancient woodland sites (or PAWS as they are known) back to native woodland (and also to encourage private woodland owners to do the same). The project is being driven by the fact that protecting and improving the ecological and social values of woodlands (in other words, how interesting they are to visit and how much good they do in terms of landscape and water catchment management) is now just as much a priority for the Forestry Commission as is the production of timber.

Already, a number of large-scale restoration projects, like that in South Yorkshire, have taken place. The exciting thing is that given a bit of help, in particular the removal of non-native trees, native woodland can regenerate quite spectacularly.

To kick-start the national project, the Forestry Commission recently undertook an extensive survey in England to find out exactly how much ancient and semi-ancient woodland they had on the land in their care. It found that about 53,000 hectares of ancient woodlands remain, while there are a further 35,426 hectares of PAWS. Overall this means that 40% of all PAWS in Britain are in the expert hands of the Forestry Commission. It also means that the Ancient Woodland Project heralds an exciting new chapter in forestry in Britain.

The conversion of PAWS to native woodland is a long-term project that will, in most cases, be carried out by thinning and replanting plantations over a number of decades. The prize will be a much more diverse mixture of wildflowers and wildlife in our woods and forests and then perhaps the people of these re-wooded isles will be really proud of this, their national forest.

Badgers, wood mice, shrews, voles, stoats, weasels and dormice all have paws and the more PAWS the Forestry Commission nurses back into broad-leaf glory, the more of all of them there will be soft-footing the countryside back into a working balance.

For further information, please see the website at:
www.forestry.gov.uk

TRUSTING IN WOODLANDS

Putting woods on your doorstep

The Millennium was celebrated in many different ways but, if you didn't take part in the Woodland Trust's 'Woods on Your Doorstep' project, you missed out on something very exciting, a project that could still be around in another thousand years' time.

In the five or so years before 2000, the Trust started the creation of 250 new woods for people and wildlife to enjoy. Two hundred of these are in England and Wales and 50 in Northern Ireland. Overall, 1.5 million trees were planted on 3,000 acres, a massive project not just in the scale of planting but in the number of people involved. To complete its goal, the Trust worked with over a quarter of a million people, many of them volunteers like you, and with hundreds of different partner organisations.

The germ of the idea for the project came out of a wood creation scheme in Cambridgeshire, which showed just what was possible when local people got really interested. By 1997, there were ten new woods in Cambridgeshire and the Trust had gained the expertise and inspiration to try something bigger.

With the backing of the Millennium Commission, 'Woods on Your Doorstep' became one of their 'national umbrella projects' that inspired the nation.

Sites between 1 and 20 acres were found by public nomination with the help of local authorities and estate agents. The suitability of each was assessed and grass roots meetings were held to gauge local feelings and gain community support. All was not plain sailing; indeed, one in every ten sites was rejected because all the local vibes were not quite right.

Funds for each project came from local authority and other grants, from local companies and particularly from local fundraising efforts. The design of the woods involved local people, organisations and schools, while the actual planting was done by contractors, with a lot of help from volunteers.

One good example of this ground-breaking project in action is 'The Jockies', Garway Hill in Herefordshire. This beautiful site has many interesting features such as fern-covered rocky dells and ancient boundary trees. The site was just 20 minutes' walk from the local village hall and the community participated in the design and planting of the new wood, a real millennium landmark.

It's not just 250 new doorstep woods, the Trust is busy with other kinds of habitat too. There are now scores of new ponds, marshes and meadows and many kilometres of managed hedgerows. Most of these new oases of biodiversity are in their infancy and tending to their needs as they mature over the years will be very exciting. What wildflowers, birds, animals and insects will turn up on your doorstep?

Even more exciting is the idea that some of their future day-to-day management may be taken over by the local communities that helped to make them. Just think; a sort of living extension to the village hall, a resource used for all sorts of things from healthful exercise to fieldwork and rural studies, all helping to put the value of biodiversity at the centre of local government.

This, of course, means that there is still a lot of work to be done – time for you to join in. Oh, and if there is not a wood on your doorstep, it's time to do something about it!

For further information, please see the website at:
www.woodland-trust.org.uk

TREES FOR LIFE

Volunteers help re-forest the glens

The New Forest, Sherwood and the Caledonian are three of our great forests that most people have heard about. Sadly, all are but a shadow of their former selves and are in need of your help.

But if you go down to a certain glen today, you'll be in for a big, pleasant surprise. You'll have stumbled on the volunteers of Trees for Life, a charity based at Findhorn Bay in the north east of Scotland. For over 15 years they have been working to regenerate and restore the native Caledonian Forest to an ever-larger area of the Scottish Highlands.

"We seek not only to counteract centuries of deforestation, but to be pioneers in the newly-emerging field of ecological restoration," says Trees for Life's founder Alan Watson Featherstone. Alan goes on to explain that the group's work is all about giving nature a "helping hand" so that the natural regeneration of this ancient and unique ecosystem can take place again.

Trees for Life funds its work through grants, donations and the sale of merchandise such as their annual, very beautiful, calendars and diaries. However, its work would be impossible without an army of volunteers who come and work hard from all over the world and return home inspired to come again or to continue the vision of landscape restoration in other places.

The Caledonian Forest originally covered much of the Highlands of Scotland – it took its name from the Romans, who called Scotland 'Caledonia', meaning 'wooded heights'. Over the centuries, the forest shrank as the human population grew. Large areas were felled to satisfy the needs of industry, while the widespread introduction of sheep and a large increase in the numbers of red deer ensured that, once the forest was cleared, it did not return.

Today, less than 1% of the original forest survives, and the native pinewoods have been reduced to a number of mostly small, isolated remnants. These remnants are running out of time, as most of them now consist only of a few old trees in a heavily-grazed landscape.

Trees for Life has a threefold strategy to make the return of the forest happen. First, it makes the natural regeneration of the trees possible, by putting up deer fences so that seedlings can grow naturally, without being over-grazed. "This is the simplest and best method of regenerating the forest, as it involves the minimum of intervention and allows nature to do most of the work," says Alan.

Where there are no existing sources of seed, Trees for Life plants native trees. It uses seed from the nearest surviving stands to maintain the local genetic variation in the forest.

The third cornerstone of regeneration is the removal of non-native trees, which in some areas have prevented the regeneration of the Caledonian Forest remnants.

Overall, Trees for Life is working to restore the forest to a contiguous area of about 600 square miles, and it is working well. Already, several hundred thousand naturally regenerating native trees have been protected from over-grazing and almost half a million Scots pines and native broad-leaves have been planted.

They work in partnership with both Forest Enterprise and the National Trust for Scotland, mainly in Glen Affric where the best ancient forest remnants still survive. Current work includes a forest restoration project on the Achlain Estate in Glen Moriston, where the group has received support from the local landowner.

Trees for Life is a model for other forest restoration projects around the world. "We believe that ecological restoration, or the healing of the Earth, must become a global priority," says Alan. "The capacity of the Earth to support life, both human and animals and plants alike, has been substantially diminished by industrial civilisation in recent decades," he explains. "Now we need to reverse that process, to restore the planet's ability to sustain abundant life, to secure our own future and that of millions of other species."

For further information, please see the website at:
www.treesforlife.org.uk

ENGLAND'S COMMUNITY FORESTS

Forests for communities, by communities

Rye Hill Colliery and its spoil tips and works, like many other similar sites in the north east of England, lay derelict for years following the demise of mining in the area. Now, however, the area has been brought back to life – by people planting trees. Rye Hill is now an extensive area of attractive countryside containing woodland, meadow, water and wetland – known as Rainton Meadows Country Park. Under the management of the local Wildlife Trust, it has become a major resource for recreation, education and contact with nature for local urban communities. Rainton Meadows is part of the Great North Forest – just one of twelve Community Forests that are bringing the magic of trees and woodlands to some of the most blighted and run-down parts of Britain.

From the Great North Forest in Tyne & Wear and Durham to the Forest of Avon around Bristol, England's Community Forests is an up-and-running programme that is reconnecting people with their local countryside. Each of the 12 forests is a local partnership between the Countryside Agency, Forestry Commission, local authorities and other stakeholders, including landowners.

"The main challenge has been driving change in the landscape," says John Vaughan, Group Director of the National Community Forest Partnership. "We have to persuade farmers to put their land under woodland and convince local authorities that some brownfield sites can be vastly improved with woodland planting."

One area where the project has had loads of support has been the involvement of volunteers from the local community. Many thousands of people have already lent a hand and groups such as the British Trust for Conservation Volunteers, Wildlife Trusts, the Woodland Trust and Groundwork are closely involved in the work and the training.

Visionary stuff, creating multi-purpose forests close to where people live and work – forests that people can enjoy, forests that soften and restore industrialised and neglected landscapes and forests that bring biodiversity back to the bits of Britain that need it most.

With over 25,000 hectares of woodlands already protected and improved and around 10,000 hectares of new woodlands planted, the impact on the landscape and its wildlife cannot be underestimated.

John explains that even in the early years of new tree planting we frequently see an explosion of species like grey partridge, brown hare and short-eared owls, small mammals and insects making use of the cover and the open ground around. With a bit of cover marvels happen.

Local knowledge and a patchwork of correct planting and management is the key. For example, in the Mersey Forest a project is being run that aims to help to reverse the national decline in the English bluebell population. With the help of schools and community groups, new areas of bluebells are being created in the forest. In fact, the Mersey Forest is one of the only places where deliberate new sowings have been made to promote the recovery of this species. However, the scheme goes beyond this – it also aims to protect existing bluebell woodlands from bulb thieves by creating a new and sustainable supply of bluebell bulbs for legitimate resale.

A survey carried out by Plantlife International to mark Her Majesty the Queen's Jubilee, asking people to nominate their favourite wildflower found in their county, put the bluebell as a firm national favourite. A good choice for, believe it or not, these islands can boast to be the native home of almost half the bluebells of the world.

Overall, the 12 Community Forests probably represent one of the best attempts at building links between the urban masses and the countryside, as they bring the healing power of trees into industrialised

Britain and allow those people who have little access to nature a chance to walk in woodland.

For further information, please see the Community Forest website at: www.communityforest.org.uk

Chapter 5

WATERS OF LIFE

WASTE NOT, WANT NOT

Stand on top of Ben Nevis with the tang of the Isles wetting your hair and you will discover just how important your eyebrows are in terms of personal environmental protection. However, what will not be so immediately apparent is that even those drops of mist have already felt the sting of change in our wider environment. Yes, even on top of Britain, those mist drops will be slightly more acidic thanks in part to NOx pouring out of our exhaust pipes and will contain a smidgen of particulate diesel from the same source.

So it's Gortex-covered backs to the sea breezes as we take the high road downhill to the lowlands. The view as we descend is stunning, but as we chase the raindrops – be they Scottish mist or Pennine mizzle – down towards the sea, we soon come across damaging changes to the balance of the catchment.

Peat cuttings and the drainage ditches that go with them become ever more numerous and ever more effective in speeding the water down from the hills, especially in those areas given over to alien conifers. This so exacerbates the effects of summer droughts and winter floods that our streams and rivers have been restrained and retrained, often with concrete, to soften the blow.

Hydro-power raised its promising head many years ago but even this doyen of alternatives (if it is of the right size and in the right place) only works at its most efficient for around 35% of the year. Even in our temperate climate, the downstream effects on our freshwater fisheries have been dire. Fish ladders certainly help and make great tourist attractions but not all fish have learned to climb ladders and the fluctuations in water temperature certainly do not help the survival of some species. Add to this the change in speed of river flow, either scouring out or silting up the main spawning areas, and the balance of our rivers goes down the drain.

Rank signs of over-grazing by sheep, cattle, horses, deer, goats and rabbits follow us all the way down the hillside, heralding a reduction in biodiversity and an increase in potential erosion and eutrophication. Eutrophication is the enrichment of water by phosphate and nitrate, which now starts at the top and gets more and more problematical en route. What climber cannot say that he or she hasn't joined the sheep eutrofying our mountain slopes while getting rid of water? While in the drier lowlands, abstraction of water to supply our ever greater demands makes matters worse. Once-famous trout-streams have disappeared and others in summer are as dry as proverbial ditch-water, while some of our lowland reservoirs are choked with the rotting remains of blue-green algal blooms, some of which are highly toxic.

Fortunately, most of these problems are being tackled in both high and low places and, in Britain, you can't get much lower in topographical terms than the fenland of East Anglia. This is the bread-and-chips basket of the British Isles and much of this, our richest farmland, is only just kept head above water by continuous pumped drainage. The effluent water from all these pumps, charged with all the chemicals known to the agriculture industry, flows on until it 'all comes out in the Wash'.

Restoring the fens

In 1986, Andrew Green decided to transform 150 acres of his Cambridgeshire arable farm into a wetland fit for wildlife. Work began in 1995 and, today, what was once drained, cultivated fenland soil is now home to marsh-harriers, bitterns, hundreds of wintering wildfowl and over 300 species of plants (see page 115).

The Kingfishers Bridge project lies in the fertile fens of East Anglia, just three kilometres away from Wicken Fen, Britain's oldest official Nature Reserve. The drainage and subsequent cultivation of the fens that started in earnest from the 1600s onwards reduced its wetland habitats to a trickle of their former selves. This once vast, head-just-above-water resource of fish and fowl that sustained a vibrant economy of marsh-men and women was systematically reduced to isolated islands. Important wildlife corridors were cut and the rich reed-beds that helped keep the waters pure and many people employed were replaced by well-fertilised monocrops. In all, 99% of all the fenland was destroyed and we have all benefited from the fact by being able to eat home-grown food.

Many tiny areas of wet fen did survive but, as drainage took its toll and as the rich peatland soils wasted away, they came under increasing threat. Wicken Fen is the most famous – a jewel of biodiversity set in an increasingly monotonous and dry arable landscape. No wonder that it became our first National Nature Reserve in 1899 and was soon acquired by the National Trust. For those who think that this august body only looks after stately homes and other buildings, you are wrong. They are among the biggest managers of land for nature conservation and own over 600 miles of the best bits of the coastline of England and Wales. Right from the start they had a real problem with Wicken Fen, for it stuck out like a sore thumb in the middle of well-drained farmland, so they had to install pumps to keep it wet.

Re-wetting Wicken Fen

Learning in part from their near-neighbours at Kingfishers Bridge, now the National Trust has set about increasing the area of wetland around their property (and, if you are a member, it is yours to visit or to volunteer to take part in this experiment) by 1,000%. However, the National Trust is not the only non-government organisation with its sights set on re-wetting fenland. Further south in the Cambridgeshire fens, the Wildlife Trust is planning to do that to

7,500 acres of erstwhile arable land in its Great Fens Project. This enormous area centres on Woodwalton Fen, donated to the organisation that was then called the Society for the Promotion of Nature Reserves in 1919 by Sir Charles Rothschild. Not far away, another great chunk is going back underwater thanks to the RSPB. No wonder the bitterns are booming.

Farmer Green, mastermind of the Kingfisher Bridge project, building on the experience of King Canute, has shown that it can be done. Canute, as you know, was unable to live up to his spin doctor's claims of turning the tide, so he set about the job of digging and burning fenland peat to keep his people warm in the teeth of the little ice age. The result was a multimillion-pound holiday resource we know today as the Norfolk Broads. Yes, those open stretches of water so many of us have learned to sail on are sites of industrial dereliction, old peat mines to be exact. All this by accident and with the help of nothing more than iron spades; no wonder we are now cashing in on the experience using all manner of mechanical diggers.

It was not all plain sailing, even in the case of the Norfolk Broads. Back in the 1950s –with millions of holidaymakers messing about in boats whose sewage systems were far from closed circuit, and farmers doing what the CAP told them to do – the balance of nature in Broadland took a turn for the worse. Swimmable waters overflowing with wildflowers and wildlife became a health hazard for holidaymakers and aquatic life alike. Thank goodness the warning bells rang in time and, with thousands of jobs at stake, good practice became the way ahead. One by one, the Broads are being brought back to life.

The cost of cleaning them up and keeping them clean is an enormous ongoing burden and the right mix of how to pay for it all still has to be found.

Wetlands teem with wildlife, adding greatly to their value as visitor attractions – a very important source of local and national income. To stand mesmerised as a marsh-harrier soars overhead, a dragonfly darts among the reeds and sedges chased by a hobby, or to experience the thrill as a fish tugs at the bait cast in or on the water, are experiences that many of us wish to have and privileges for which many of us are prepared to pay. Tourism and recreation are valuable sources of the currency needed to recreate or sustain the landscape of the fens, as are the incentive payments made by the UK government to farmers who voluntarily agree to raise their water levels and allow fenland vegetation to take root once more.

Our wetlands are sanctuaries for wildlife and wetland habitats are among the most productive resources on earth. But wetlands also act like giant sponges, taking in water when there is a surplus and slowly and steadily releasing it, thus ameliorating the devastating effects of both flooding and drought. Combined with their ability to slow down the rate at which water flows, thus encouraging sediments and minerals to settle out, wetlands have a major part to play in maintaining a constant, reliable supply of clean, fresh water. Although water quality in the UK has steadily improved since 1990, the amount of water abstracted from UK surface and groundwater sources has also risen since the mid-1990s, making fresh water an increasingly scarce resource that depends now, more than ever, upon the buffering effects of extensive wetlands to prevent it from drying up altogether.

The sad fact is that many water-tables are now in, or threatened with, draw down thanks to overuse and abstraction. Indeed, many of our once-lowland trout-streams now dry up in the summer, while pick-your-own summer fruits and other crops are being watered in the most wasteful way by spray irrigation. Most of our village ponds have gone and many ditches are concrete-lined or underground in pipes.

Stand-pipes and water metering may be annoying but the drying up of our rivers and wetlands is a much greater catastrophe, especially as it exacerbates the concentration of any pollutants that are in the water. The demand for water for domestic and industrial use, for agriculture and aquaculture, must be reined in if we are not to see further loss of the nation's rivers and wetlands and the fish and other animals they support.

The case rests that the more water we waste, the more problems we will have in maintaining a viable countryside and a viable economy. We must also be careful not to become dependent on food supplies from other countries, even the USA, for they are running out of irrigation water too.

Protecting the rivers

Sadly, our rivers and estuaries have long been regarded by humans as convenient dumping grounds for waste of all sorts. A flowing river may carry a pollution problem out of sight but it inconveniently dumps it in someone else's backyard; so much so that rivers like London's Wandle, a tributary of the Thames, were even designated as sewers as late as the 1960s. Many post-war years of poisoning, by industrial pollution or eutrophication by agricultural run-off and sewage discharge, produced rivers that more closely resembled lifeless drains than natural watercourses. Thankfully, a variety of local, national and international initiatives introduced in recent years have produced improvements in the quality of Britain's river water, with the benefits being felt by both people and wildlife (see page 118).

In October 2000, the Water Framework Directive was published by the EU Parliament, which requires all EU member states to put into place systems for managing all their water environments. That is all rivers, lochs, lakes, estuaries and coastal waters, as well as water underground: exciting new legislation based on natural river basin districts. Even more exciting, this 'river-basin management' approach must be supported by extensive environmental monitoring and scientific investigation, and must not only achieve its targets of 'good ecological status' by 2015, but must also encourage the sustainable use of water resources.

Although the Water Framework Directive is concerned with water, its scope requires consideration of any human action on the land in a water catchment area that could affect the quality of that water. The environmental objectives by which the progress of a particular river basin management plan can be assessed will be based on ecology, meaning that the plants and animals living in our watercourses and wetlands will become the indicators of the quality of the water environment. The simple truth is that if they are thriving, then the quality of the water must be good!

Clean water is vital to life but, in many parts of Britain, it is an asset that contributes millions of pounds to the local economy each year as tourists flood in to pursue the nation's most popular sport – fishing.

As London's Wandle Valley mapping project has shown, by instilling in the younger generation a fascination and respect for their local rivers and the fish population within them, these living assets can be safeguarded and improved for the future. Likewise, the salmon in the classroom project that the Galloway Fisheries Trust has run each year since 1991 in their local primary schools, educates the children in the life-cycle of the Atlantic salmon and the environmental problems faced by this species. Hatching salmon eggs in specially-constructed tanks in the classroom and then releasing the fry into their local burn helps the children to understand the value of their local environment, especially clean water, and to appreciate the important role sport-fishing plays in the local economy. Any scheme that helps develop environmental and social responsibility is to be applauded and encouraged.

Sustainable management of our wetland habitats – our lakes, rivers, marshes, estuaries and peatlands – represents our only hope of safeguarding supplies of freshwater and wetland biodiversity. But this isn't a new idea. In 1971, the late Sir Peter Scott, founder of the Wildfowl and Wetlands Trust, championed the International Convention on Wetlands of International Importance "especially as Water Fowl Habitats" at its launch in Ramsar in Iran. This inter-governmental treaty, now know as the RAMSAR Convention, has provided the framework within which countries can adopt national action and international co-operation for the conservation and wise use of wetlands and their resources. Today, there are over 1,000 RAMSAR wetland sites in 116 countries, with 169 in Britain, emphasising this country's global significance for the conservation of wetland habitats. Our challenge is to learn from our mistakes of the past and to manage Britain's many wetland habitats, both natural and man-made, back into more natural working order for the benefit of people and wildlife. The good news is that it is happening.

A BLOOMING AND A BOOMING SUCCESS

Putting the wetland back

There are several reasons why Andrew Green decided to create 160 acres of wetland habitat on his farm in Cambridgeshire. For a start he enjoys a challenge, likes birds and wet feet. Apart from that, everything about the site screamed out that it was the right place to have a go.

Andrew's farm contained land ideal to be returned into well-managed reed-beds once again. It is adjacent to the washlands of the River Cam, themselves in great need of expansion to accommodate migrating wildfowl. It is also on one of the major trans-Britain flyways between the Wash and the Severn Estuary.

The site is next to the Upware North Pit SSSI and only three kilometres from the National Trust's reserve at Wicken Fen. So here was a 'grass is greener' showcase site if ever there was one, tempting other groups and individuals to have a go, including those farmers who, due to wastage of the organic component of their soils, were finding it ever harder to make the economic grade.

Since 1995, the Kingfishers Bridge Wetland Creation Project has transformed 65 hectares of arable farmland into a mosaic of wildlife habitats. Former potato and cereal fields are now reed-beds, fens, ditches, ponds, streams, islands, meadows, wader scrapes and cliffs supporting a great diversity of wetland plants and animals. The site benefits from a variety of water sources, and water levels at the site are carefully managed for optimum wildlife benefit, with the use of banks, ditches and sluices.

The project was started as a private initiative by Andrew, whose family own the site at Wicken. From its inception, the site has attracted widespread interest for the diversity of water birds it attracts, its vegetational succession and species recovery programmes.

"The wildlife is thriving in variety and numbers," enthuses Andrew. "Bitterns bred for the first time in a newly-created wetland here last year, and we hope they will do so again next year – I saw one yesterday at five metres!" The only thing that really surprised him was how quickly it all happened.

The project's wildlife success owes much to the partnership between Andrew and Roger Beecroft, a wildlife consultant who managed the creation of the Trimley reserve at Felixstowe and who has helped to plan and manage the Kingfishers Bridge project since 1965. The results are perhaps best illustrated by the amazing story of how the very rare water germander now flourishes in the restored fenland habitat at Kingfishers Bridge.

The Upware North Pit SSSI is a former limestone quarry lying in land belonging to Andrew and his sons adjacent to the Kingfishers Bridge project area. The Upware North Pit was the only site in eastern England where 12 remaining individuals of the water germander survived and only one of three known locations in the whole of Britain. With the help of some funding from English Nature's Species Recovery Programme, plants propagated from those growing at the Upware site were soon doing well in the recreated fenland sites in August 1998. The results have been staggering, with the populations of water germander on Andrew's land now standing at over 50,000 – an increase of over 400,000%!

The Kingfishers Bridge Wetland Creation Trust was set up in 1999 to support the conservation and management of the area for the maximum benefit of wildlife. The site is primarily a wildlife sanctuary and as that it is a stunning success, but funding has not been a matter of plain sailing.

"As a private venture, we are unable to access the big environmental funds, such as the four million pounds that are available for projects to enhance bittern populations, via the RSPB, and it is increasingly difficult to manage such ambitious projects as ours. While a welcome small lottery grant has enabled the addition of a number of new habitats together with important improvement to the reed-bed environment, we mainly live in hope, which is fortunately quite cheap at the moment!"

Let us hope that sufficient support from the friends of the project, together with a future corporate sponsor with a strong interest in wildlife and conservation research, can be found to help keep this shining example of wetland habitat restoration and management afloat.

For more information, please see the website at: www.kfbweb.info

WIND IN THE WANDLE

Trout in the classroom

Three hundred years ago, the River Wandle, a tributary of the River Thames, was a crystal-clear chalk stream, a great place to catch wild salmon and brown trout. Then came the industrial revolution and soon the Wandle was one of the most hard-worked rivers in the country, its waters impounded by weirs so that they could be used again and again to drive the water wheels of industry. Sadly, it also became a dumping ground for the waste produced not only by the 90 factories but also by the rapidly-growing human population of the area. A real public convenience which was given the official title of 'sewer' in the 1960s! Not surprisingly, the trout and salmon, together with the rest of the wildlife, were driven out of the river, but not forever…

Massive work by Thames Water paved the way and, in 1995, based on a community-wide survey of the river, the JetSet Club came into being. This environmental task force was set up to promote, conserve, protect and improve the physical and natural environment of the Wandle Valley, by involving local communities in this process, especially the young people of Wandsworth, Merton, Sutton and Croydon. Thanks to the vision and energy of the club's founder and co-ordinator, Alan Suttie, all of the organisations that are responsible for the health of the Wandle are now working together to nurse the river back into biodiverse working order.

The reward for all this hard work is that the river is now fit for trout and salmon to return and, in March 2003, members of the JetSet Club released the first of thousands of young brown trout into the Wandle. A real green letter day for all concerned and an amazing achievement – a first for brown trout in the UK.

Even more remarkable is the fact that brown trout fry that will be released over the next ten years will be raised by local school children. Thanks to a grant from the Abela Foundation, 20 schools from nursery to sixth form all along the Wandle Valley will have high-tech aquarium tanks in their classrooms. Brown trout eggs, supplied under licence from the Environment Agency, will be nurtured into fry by the children as they learn about the ecology of their river. Then, with great ceremony, the fry will be released into the Wandle at a point close to the school that hatched them.

All concerned hope that this will help to rekindle a sense of place and responsibility in the local population. Then perhaps the JetSet Club will not continually have to remove litter from their patch. Wishful thinking? Well, already decisions are being taken in the highest places to rethink development that could preclude opening up stretches of the Wandle now hidden underground. Half a mile of chalk stream will once again sparkle on its way through Croydon.

If that's not good news enough, how about the fact that, thanks to another great partnership of like-minded people centred on the Environment Agency and Thames Water, Old Father Thames himself has been given the aquatic facelift of all time – enough to be dubbed 'the cleanest river flowing through any capital city in Europe'. No wonder that in the millennium year he could come out smiling from under the wobbly bridge and past the dome as he flowed on down to the sea. Five years on (in the year of the 300th anniversary of the Battle of Trafalgar), Horatio Nelson, who fished the Wandle in its prime, will be able to look down on another battle well won.

For more information, please see the website at:
www.jet-set.org.uk

WHOLES AMONG FRIENDS

Visiting the Cotswold Waterpark

Flying into Heathrow from the west, you can look down on a wonderland of lakes, replete with people messing about in boats or watching the birds. Without doubt, the showcase is the Wildfowl and Wetlands Trust Barn Elms Reservoir development. To get there you can take the 'Duck Bus' from Hammersmith Station to enjoy the spectacle of a cross-section of the world's wildfowl floating about on what was once London's water supply. The rest of the new lakes are much more natural and are all there thanks to the hard work of the extractive industries.

Water is the basis of life and aggregates are the basis of civil engineering, itself the foundation of civilisation as we know it and that means digging holes somewhere in the countryside.

Well-designed buildings, hospitals, homes, sea defences, roads and railways surely do have certain environmental advantages and, without lime, much of even the organic agricultural land of the world would be unproductive. What is more, over a third of the nature reserves and SSSIs (Sites of Special Scientific Interest) in Britain are old quarries and gravel-pits.

Some of the best I know about were close to the headwaters of the River Thames, where half a century of gravel and sand extraction had created an enormous people-made lake wetland complex. A fantastic opportunity seized on by Mother Nature, who did her best to heal the wounds in the most biodiverse way possible. Just a few years ago, one of the best days of my life was spent in and around one of the 150-plus lakes and there are more being dug all the time. Checking the water plants, especially the stoneworts, I knew that the water was both swimmable and drinkable. In I went as two grass snakes shot off in front of me. After drinking my fill, I floated on my back, spouting water into the air as a hobby came down and caught a big dragonfly just above my head. Absolutely fabulous, just like the Norfolk Broads were in my youth.

When I first heard about the proposed development of the Cotswold Water Park, my heart, like those of many locals, sank. All that traffic congesting all those country roads, all those noisy water-skiers and jet boats – what a terrible thing to do to such an important part of the rural headwaters of the Thames.

Well, it happened and some of those things did come to pass but something magical has also taken place. The Cotswold Water Park Society came into existence and, thanks in great part to their vision and expertise, a harmony of understanding and pulling together is working wonders. It's a blooming marvellous place for water and land-based holidays but it's also of national and international importance – a showcase for getting the formula right. The Cotswolds' own international multipurpose Nature Reserve in the making.

Now with the new park biodiversity plan (a co-operative effort between English Nature, Gloucestershire Wildlife Trust, the Environment Agency, the Wildfowl and Wetlands Trust, Cotswold District Council, CWP Joint Committee, Cotswold Water Park Society Limited, Wiltshire Ornithological Society, Sand and Gravel Association, BACMI, ARC Southern and the National Farmers Union – a biodiverse group if ever there was one), it's all stations go for a better, greener, self-financing future.

Every time I make a visit, and I always do when I am in the vicinity, there is something new to see which links environmental care with nature conservation. Happy healthy holidays for all the family, with environmental education and sustainable land use on tap. All good potable news from the headwaters of Old Father Thames – I have to say it again – now the cleanest river flowing through any capital city in Europe.

For more information, please see the website at:
www.waterpark.org

THE RIVER TWEED

Not just a fisherman's tale!

Unlike most fishing tales, there is no need to embroider this particular story, because it is the best news to come out of Scotland's rivers for many a long fishing season. The 10,300 rod catches of wild salmon made by fishermen on the River Tweed in 2002 represented the best landings for a decade, and gave the river the reputation of being the most productive salmon river in the North Atlantic system. When the data for 2003 became available, no-one could believe the figures. The 13,888 salmon caught in the Tweed using rod and line during that season is the best catch result since records began in 1963, and probably represents an all-time high!

This is all the more incredible because, like most salmon rivers flowing into the North Atlantic, the Tweed has been going through bad times.

In the old days, the mature salmon would return to the rivers of their birth, many perhaps to exactly the same stretch of river – the same intensive care unit from which they and their parents had set out in life. There they would mate and lay their eggs in gravel washed clean with the purest of water, fully charged with oxygen. The fittest adults would then make their way back down to the sea and some would return real whoppers: the record fish of a not-so-distant past, before Gortex had been invented and the tweedy set mostly wore tweeds. The less fit would die in those upland streams, their rotting bodies enriching the habitat with the right nutrients, not too little, not too much, ensuring there was plenty of food for their progeny.

In many rivers today, the fish returning to their traditional spawning grounds are caught and stripped of their eggs and sperm. These are mixed willy-nilly and the progeny are raised in hatcheries before being released to restock the river. Gone is their sense of place and gone is the sensibility of natural history, the very essence of a balanced river.

The River Tweed Commissioners, the body responsible for the preservation and increase of salmon, sea trout, trout and other freshwater fish in the River Tweed and its tributaries, believe that management practices initiated by the Tweed Foundation 15 years ago are largely responsible for the improved catches. Central to the Tweed Foundation's philosophy for the management of the river is their belief that if the fish have access to as much spawning territory as possible, and if the environmental conditions in the spawning and nursery streams maximise the production and survival of the wild juvenile fish stocks, their populations will thrive and restocking of the rivers will not be necessary.

Catch-release schemes, where anglers return a significant number of caught salmon to the river unharmed, have helped to boost the numbers of mature salmon reaching the headwaters of the Tweed to spawn, as has £2 million of investment in conservation measures which have helped to open up all channels to migrating salmon returning to their Borders spawning grounds.

Combined with enhancement of the fish habitat within the Tweed's catchment as a whole, the measures have allowed the natural, sustainable regeneration of the Tweed's wild salmon stocks. Closure of the north east of England's drift-net fishery and reduced coastal and estuary netting, paid for in great part by fishing enthusiasts, have also increased the likelihood of the River Tweed's wild salmon finding their way upstream to their age-old spawning grounds unimpeded.

The reward for the huge commitment of resources that local fisheries proprietors have made to pay for all these improvements is not only the return of that sense and sensibility to the river. There has also been a radical upward revision of the value of wild salmon rod-fishing on the Tweed to the local economy, which currently stands at least at £13 million per year!

The knock-on effect of this amazing story is enormous: if you can do it on the Tweed, the world is your swan mussel, if not your oyster. (Swan mussels are nature's own solar-powered water cleansers and their diminutive cousins still produce freshwater pearls in our cleanest waters.)

Good news travels fast, especially through the glens of Scotland. Working together, the Strathclyde Police and East Renfrewshire Council have launched their Angling for Youth and Development (AYFD) scheme that aims to introduce youngsters to the delights of fly-fishing in their own community. The scheme's broad-based courses don't just lead to Scottish Vocational Qualifications, they also aim to nurture a lifelong sense of responsibility for the well-being of their local rivers and the fish populations that they support.

Just to show that it's not only the boys and girls in blue who are keen to tackle the issue of attitudes of the young to environmental responsibility, Breadalbane Academy has taken up the challenge with courses in the art of being a ghillie or a gamekeeper, leading to accreditation for SVQs. Meanwhile, a hub site is being developed in Fife and Tayside, with a Countryside Educational Centre built around four disused gravel-pits.

For more information, please see the website at: www.rtc.org.uk

WATER VOLE RE-INTRODUCTIONS

More tails on the riverbank

When Kenneth Grahame's book *The Wind in the Willows* was published in 1908, his characters were everyday countryside creatures, familiar to all and instantly recognisable from his engaging descriptions. Almost a century later, how the story has changed!

Mole may still play the part of the industrious, secretive digger, and Toad's fatal attraction for the motor-car continues to get him into so much trouble that humans have to help him across the road in the spring. Otherwise he could be flattened before he could reach the spawning pond! However, poor old Ratty (who isn't a rat at all but a water vole) has almost been written out of the story.

Why? Because he's lost much of his beloved riverside home, food and water supply to intensive agriculture, water abstraction and other riverside developments. He is also being poisoned by people who can't tell the difference between water voles and brown rats. Furthermore, both he and all the other 'ratties' have been persecuted, and in places wiped out, by a murderous character that wasn't even living on the British riverbank in Kenneth Grahame's day, the North American mink.

Things became so bad for the water vole that its UK population plummeted by 90% from over seven million in 1989 to less than 900,000 in 1996. In the south west of England, its population declined by 97% during that period. This alarming state of affairs prompted action in partnership across the UK to halt the eradication of this species.

For the past five years, Bristol Zoo Gardens has been breeding water voles successfully for re-introduction purposes, helping to re-establish viable water vole populations on the Kennet and Avon Canal near Bath.

In April 2003, the project extended its range into the North Somerset Levels, where water voles were believed to be extinct. 64 captive-bred water voles were released into the wild in a suitable mink-free habitat, just outside Bristol, where the partners in the scheme – Bristol Zoo Gardens, the Environment Agency, the Hawk and Owl Trust, Landmark Environmental Consultants and the landowners, as well as volunteers from the Yatton and Congresbury Wildlife Action Group and the North Somerset Wildlife Wardens – hoped they could establish a thriving water vole population.

All the water voles were health-checked by the zoo's vets before release. They were provided with temporary riverside homes, in the form of food-filled holding pens, out of which they could burrow once they felt ready to dig themselves a home of their own in the riverbank. 15 of the voles were fitted with specially-designed radio collars, vital to monitoring how well the water voles were settling into their new riverside abodes.

So successfully have the animals established themselves in this new area that six months and several litters per female water vole later, surveys put their numbers at between 300 and 400! Bristol Zoo's overseer of small mammals, Simon Eyre, attributes the success of the zoo's water vole breeding and re-introduction programme to teamwork. "This re-introduction could not have taken place, let alone be doing as well as it appears to be, without the partnerships and volunteer team that that have been formed for this project."

Continued monitoring of the population will be vital if these riverside characters are to escape the predatory mink, but there is now hope that, thanks to a spirit of co-operation, water voles in some of the country's riverbanks may enjoy the tranquil, mink-free existence that Kenneth Grahame's Ratty did back in 1908.

For more information, please see the website at:
www.bristolzoo.org.uk

Chapter 6

THE SEA AROUND US

WALLOPING THE COD

Almost 40 years ago I became an environmental campaigner on the fish front in my favourite chippy. The lady who fried them to perfection asked me this question: "Why is it that half the world are starving and half the world are slimming?" I hid my inadequate answer behind a copy of the *Daily Mirror* that, in those now far-off days, was allowed to be used as a container for my second helping of cod. Cod is today an endangered species along with the once very common eel, both of which I have now had to cut out from my diet.

The latter was a hard decision for an old East Ender, for eels, though reviled by many as squiggly slimy things to be avoided at all costs, are a traditional part of the cockney diet. No more eels, jellied or smoked, and no more elver pie for me, for if the right actions are not taken, and fast, very soon there will be none for left for anybody, let alone all the animals that depend on them. The sad news is that Britain has lost 99% of its eels in the past 20 years. This is a catastrophe on the Armageddon scale, for once these amazing fish have migrated clear across the North Atlantic to the Sargasso Sea, their offspring make their way back to our shores and restock all our rivers, streams, canals, lakes, ponds and even urban ditches and saline water bodies with scrumptious eels.

It is true to say that anywhere you live in lowland Britain there's an eel feeding or being eaten by an animal in your nearest body of water, even in your nearest pond. At least it is probably still true, but for every hundred that were about their important business in the 1980s there is only one today. This means the whole balance of life in our watery habitats and in the North Atlantic has changed dramatically and even our scientists don't understand exactly what is making it happen. Over-exploitation of all stages of its amazing life-cycle is certainly part of the problem and, with elvers fetching over $1,200 a kilo on the international market, you can see the problem.

Reacting to these signs, the industry has instituted farms to which elvers caught from the wild are transported so they can begin to mature out of danger of predation. But it is not enough. A complete cessation of eel catching in any form would appear to be part of the answer but, as we do not know the full story, any politician would be loath to throw in his lot and his livelihood behind such legislation.

Adding to the eel's problems is the fact that recently an exotic parasitic worm has begun to infest them. This was, in all probability, brought in sea-water used as ballast in giant tankers, each one of which is a floating aquarium harbouring long-haul immigrants, some of which can cause great trouble – like the role of a jelly fish that took over the Black Sea in recent years, helping to wipe out its rich fisheries; a sea that came into existence at about the same time as the English Channel, thanks to melting ice-caps.

Fishing too many fish

Britain became an island only 7,500 years ago, thanks to natural global warming and, from that point on, all new plants and animals arriving on our shores were officially listed as non-native, for they needed human help to make the crossing. If only grey squirrels, mink and Japanese knotweed, etc., etc. had never been given a helping hand.

The piles of oyster and other edible shellfish shells and the bones of fish that make up the bulk of ancient middens, sculptured landfill sites that litter our shores, prove that right from the start people had a dire effect on the inshore food chain. Fishing with gay abandon until the size of the catch made them move on until their rights were challenged by more advanced cultures coming the other way.

Just how many sea-birds, whales and dolphins shared residence with our ancestors back in those early days we can only guess but what a spectacle it must have been. Perhaps this is one reason that we, their descendants, do like to be beside the seaside.

Sadly, some 7,450 years later, another mass exterminator turned up on the Northern European scene: not another ice-cap but something almost as bad – a highly-subsidised CAP. As the Common Agricultural Policy started to do its worse on the land, the Common Fisheries Policy (CFP) took the battle out to sea.

I used to think that the oceans were so large that a single species, however stupid, could never cause major damage to the marine environment. How wrong could I be?

The real problem was, of course, that underwater such destruction was out of sight and so out of mind. Luckily, at about the same time, Jacques Cousteau changed all that by inventing scuba-diving. Very soon, Hans and Lotte Hass were on our screens warning of the terrible things happening below the waves and, a few years later, the 'Rainbow Warriors' of Greenpeace were campaigning to save our seas from products of nuclear reprocessing and our whales from extinction.

We tend to forget that the great auk had been bludgeoned into extinction by 1844 in Scotland and by the 1930s, because of persecution by fishermen, the European grey seal had become the rarest large mammal in the world. Its dwindling breeding population on the Farne Islands was given the protection of a special Act of Parliament. That is the main reason why today the seal population now spreads around our coast, much to the pleasure of tourists but to the annoyance of fishers, who are now demanding a massive cull.

However, although these same fishermen argue their case on the basis of unfair competition with the seals, the demise of our fishing fleets and their communities has been almost entirely due to the CFP and the fact that if you can't afford to police the countryside how can you monitor the fish quotas, let alone the by-catch? A harmless sort of word that in fact means the wanton slaughter of all other species, including birds and dolphins, that get caught up in nets or on long lines to be chucked back into the sea, mostly dead – another real mess someone has gotten us into.

The seas are a shared resource and, even if they weren't, it would be foolish to continue such rank levels of over-exploitation. Such over-fishing only continues because of the enormous subsidies some countries pay to keep the high-tech boats afloat.

We hear a lot about agricultural subsidies but little about the fact that world fisheries are also subsidised to a staggering level. According to the United Nations Food and Agricultural Organisation, in 1992, of the total $124 billion annual costs for the world fleet, $54 billion was subsidies in the form of price controls, low-interest loans, outright grants and fuel tax exemptions.

This level of subsidy not only distorts the basis of free trade in the favour of the rich but also ends in catastrophe for poor and rich alike. The time has come for subsidies to be used to monitor and enforce sustainable levels of fishing and for backing integrated inshore management.

The sad truth is that, thanks to the CFP and the massive catch quotas it allowed, several important fish stocks, such as cod, are today on the verge of collapse. This disaster has, of course, not gone unnoticed and, in 2003, the European Union got a new revised fisheries policy which promised a range of measures to maintain safe levels of adult fish in EU waters, including limiting by-catch and a clamp-down on illegal fishing.

Since then fishermen in the UK have seen the introduction of massively-reduced quotas for threatened species, stronger restrictions on the number of days that they can operate at sea and the establishment of no-take zones and fish protection zones off the west coast of Scotland and in the North Sea.

Of course, these moves have had a crippling impact on fishermen and their communities, with many boats being decommissioned and many fishermen being forced to pack up shop and sell their boats for scrap. The political fall-out has also been enormous, with newspaper headlines full of talk of the wholesale 'betrayal' of fishing communities and some fishermen threatening to break the law and land illegal catches in order to continue to make a living.

The jury is still out on whether these moves will make a lasting impact on the fish stocks in the seas around Britain, with many environmentalists already saying that, despite all the upheaval, too little is being done in the name of political expediency. It is clear that the year-on-year political haggling over how much fish each of the EU's fleets should be allowed to catch is not going to guarantee that the fish in our seas are safe.

What *is* clear is that the future sustainability of the fish stocks in our seas – and the fishing communities that depend on them – needs to be built on scientifically-informed long-term quotas. According to researchers at WWF, in the past, political pressure has led to fishing quotas being set at an average of 30% above the recommendations made by research groups, such as the International Council in the Exploration of the Seas (ICES). It is a mistake that must not be allowed to happen again.

Pollution problems

There is good news on the pollution front because, post the *Torrey Canyon*, a disaster that plastered some of our best holiday beaches with crude oil, many industries started to put their effluent houses into some sort of order, some even finding that they could boost company profit by reprocessing and selling the waste. The first positive move in the oil industry was called 'load on top', which meant that instead of flushing oily wash waters out to pollute the sea, they were contained within the ships floating on the top of the water, ready to be recycled for use once back in port.

The water companies, with the encouragement of campaigners such as sports-fishers and Surfers Against Sewage (see page 144), started to clean up their act. There is still a long way to go but things are getting better all the time. Sadly, the most insidious part of marine pollution is still there out of sight and out of mind, called eutrophication; a word that should be one of the most dreaded in twenty-first century Britain, for it is a creeping holocaust that is silently infusing both the land and the sea. As we have already seen, the enrichment of fresh water by phosphate and nitrate can really upset the balance of nature wherever it happens and from wherever the chemicals come. The same is now painfully true of the sea.

The complex interaction of all these factors is enormous. Before the present round of over-fishing of our national Friday fish dish, cod used to mature and start to reproduce at around nine years of age, when they were really big, grown-up fish. As today few, if any, live to this age, rapid natural selection has favoured the survival of precocious youngsters and most cod now mate when only three years old, when of course they are much smaller. This means that the nutrients once locked up in those large fish are now in cycle in the sea, further upsetting the balance of nutrients, while synthetic steroids and even sex hormones find their way down our rivers, further clouding the 'get the cod back' issue.

Warning bells rang along the Northumberland coast in the 1970s when five people were rushed into Newcastle Infirmary suffering from what turned out to be Toxic Mussel Poisoning. As its name suggests, this comes from eating shellfish that have themselves gorged on microscopic part-plant, part-animals living in the sea. It was almost a Spielberg scenario, for you could stand on the coast and see the Farne Islands picked out in a sea of fiery gold; a bloom of luminous microscopic plankton at least in part triggered by eutrophication. Fortunately, none of the patients died but a lot of seabirds did.

It's no good just blaming the farmers and fertiliser manufacturers because when we have made use of food of any sort, our waste is full of those nutrients often gleaned from all over the world, which we then flush down the loo. In recent times, our water companies have done wonders in cleaning up the problems caused by our number twos but, even with the bulk of the organic matter gone, the eutrophicants are still there and it costs an awful lot to strip them out. The good news is that now even that is starting to happen.

However, what about the poor old farmers: most of the spare nutrients from their fields don't come out through a single orifice but seep into streams and rivers across the field margins. This is, of course, much more difficult to deal with but, as we will see, integrated crop management and Conservation Grade farming can reduce even that load.

Fish-farms and other fishy problems

Fish-farms are another immense problem. The developers whirred up the spin doctors with glee: think of all the jobs in remote rural areas, think of non-poached salmon cheap enough to be a main course on our school menus every Friday. Why didn't they stop to think?

It was and still is a dream that the human population will one day be fed with all the fish and shellfish they need, produced in well-managed farms. To do that is not impossible, but would of course take lots of careful planning, wise management and high investment. Sadly, as economists, not ecologists, call the shots there appeared to be little or no recognition of the fact that building a large fish-farm anywhere has all the problems of building a floating village, including food supply and effluent treatment.

The answer to finding food to feed the farmed fish was big boats with big suction pumps that heralded the days of so-called industrial fishing – lots of jobs (one hoped) in the shipyards that were in fear of being closed down. Off they went, hoovering up all the little fish like sand eels and capelin for the production of meals for the fish and fish meal to be used as fertiliser, with no heed of the fact that all those little fish are important parts of the food chain that feeds other fish, sea-birds and even marine mammals, some of which are on the endangered list.

And what about all that effluent from the fish-farms? It really should have been treated as toxic waste even if it could be called organic, which it cannot, because of all the chemicals used to keep the fish healthy in those crowded cages. Instead, it was allowed to flow into some of Europe's cleanest coastal waters; meanwhile, farmed fish escaped and tainted the purity of the genetic heritage of our native salmon.

How stupid can you get? For at the same time, arguments were rife about fish quotas to protect fish stocks like the cod. Billions of pounds worth of high-tech fishing boats, with all the gear that makes them so efficient, were put in mothballs – collapsing local economies from Rockall southwards. The quotas and the mothballs were all part of a scheme to protect our fish stocks so they could begin to get back to their CFP figures. With more and more of the small fry being sucked up, what were they going to feed on? Little wonder our fishers, the few we have left, are still getting mad.

Marine energy

Of course, fishing isn't the only cause of arguments on the high seas – there's another problem on the horizon. When I first started to think about wind farms, the idea of putting them out to sea did seem a saving grace, as the wind factories would be out of bounds for fishing boats and hence the fish would be left in peace. One interesting point regarding the pro-wind farm propaganda is that they don't make much of this fact. Perhaps it's because of potential pollution from anti-foulants or perhaps it's that they just don't want any more aggro, especially from another industry whom they might see as competitors for the massive governmental subsidies they are demanding.

Already, rightly or wrongly, many fishers and shellfishers are very angry about the potential annexation of their local territory. They are not alone in worrying about this new technology. The costs of building and servicing the turbines (which would include the cost of cleaning the vanes from encrusted salt that can reduce their efficiency) are putting some investors off. This is despite the fact that it would also remove the telltale DNA that could fingerprint what birds were being killed!

Add to this the fact that the Danes – the world leaders in and exporters of wind technology – are now coming up against a raft of problems, not the least being the high cost of their electricity both to their consumers and to their economy. The recent admission that an expansion of their showcase wind farms will do little to stabilise their grid system and little or nothing to reduce their emissions of carbon dioxide would, I believe, in more normal circumstances prove the death-knell of wind power already labelled by some as bird-killing 'political electricity'.

Wind is not the only renewable energy technology threatening the seas and coastlines – barrages and the turbines they contain are another. Estuaries, which we must remember are the kidneys of the land and the ovaries of the sea, should not be impounded for any but the best of reasons. One of the reasons for saying 'no' to the proposed Severn Barrage was the possible effect on all those elvers pouring up the river on the tidal bore. Dam an estuary and you damn many species to local extinction.

In contrast to the pitfalls of wind turbines and tidal barrages, the potential of underwater turbines is awesome for, thanks to the moon, the tides wax and wane twice a day and turbines tethered in open water flip flop to catch the surge of water almost around the clock. As no impoundment is required the problems are much less. However, some latter day Jonases counsel that too many might slow the North Atlantic drift, putting us all back in the freezer.

Wave power now tested by the American Navy to replace the need for diesel in bio-diverse waters is being scaled up to ten-megawatt size. The proud boast of Ocean Power Technology, now afloat on the stock market and under contract to build its first array in Spain, is that a series of power buoy clusters strategically located in water more than 30 metres deep and covering in all a total area of 1,000 square kilometres would provide a lot of base load electricity for Europe. Out of sight but not out of mind, they would be regularly serviced by local communities, thereby providing a range of very worth-while jobs – just like the prototype now working in the Orkneys.

Britain is so well-endowed with waves that locations could be chosen far away from important hatchery and feeding grounds and as close as possible to major grid line connectors, doing away with the planning nightmare and enormous costs of new pylon routes. Surely wave power must be looked upon as an important part of sustainable development.

Non-joined-up thinking means we're all at sea

Unfortunately, there are lots of other problems – and conflicts of interest and understanding – out at sea. One image that perhaps best illustrates what I am talking about is a video of a trip out towards the Dogger Bank, taken from a submersible. The video shows the seabed shattered by the marks of beam trawls, a few broken urchin shells, rubbish of all sorts with a few tiny fish lurking, doing their best to hide in designer labelled cans. Suddenly – a straight line, replete with biodiversity! Another ten miles on or so, a boring, boring seabed paved not with sustainable gold but etched with the graffiti of big trawls. Then, another straight line with lots more marine life, including bigger fish. They look like underwater hedgerows providing food and shelter for the marine creatures but are in fact oil and gas pipelines doing exactly the same thing. Onwards, ever onwards; all of a sudden lots more fish of all shapes and sizes – surely it must be the Dogger Bank (once fabled as one of the world's great fishing grounds). No, the cameras are approaching an oil-rig, the only safe haven from the voracious fishing industry.

Because of the potential benefit rigs and their associated hardware give to undersea biodiversity, the world could never really understand why Greenpeace got their wet suits in such a twist over the decommissioning of the Brent Spar oil rig, when they had earlier campaigned for artificial reefs to give our fish a better chance of breeding. Where did Brent Spar end up? A jetty in Norway that could be used for fishing, tourism or, perish the thought, whaling under the all-embracing banner of Gro Harlem Bruntland's bright idea of sustainable development.

Super quarries and shoreline protection

Removal of anything from the seabed can cause changes to the balance of life and to the balance of erosion and deposition along the coast. When the giant dredgers of the extractive industries get going, especially near fish spawning, rearing and feeding grounds, the problems can be catastrophic with down-current effects over long distances.

Could part of the answer be sub-sea super quarries to localise the effect, like the one mooted on the Isle of Harris. There the developers, who claimed an enviable reputation for quarry restoration, in effect planned to move a cliff and ship bits of it around the world to where it was needed. Their aim was to re-landscape the hole as they went, providing new protected cliff habitats and nest sites for all the birds that use the island and which are already under great attack from mink. Some people said what a great tourist attraction that would have been, replacing the unsightly remains of a small quarry and some extremely bad examples of over-grazing with the clamour of nesting sea-birds in all their glory. And think of all the lesser quarries that would not have to be dug around the country with all the noise, dust and road traffic disturbance they cause. For some it seemed like a win-win situation; for others, the same facts spelled lose-lose. In the end we have been left with a piecemeal approach that has not provided the optimum benefit to the environment.

What of the future at sea?

The net effect of all this non-joined-up thinking has led to the fact that the seas are in such imbalance that most of the major fish stocks of the world are being fished at, and way beyond, their sustainable limit and some have collapsed.

The Australian state of Victoria is showing the way, in that over 5.5% of their coastline now comprises 'no take' fishing areas and already local fish and shellfish stocks are showing a positive response, much to the delight of the sports-fishermen, some of whom were violently opposed to the scheme. Slowly, the UK is catching on and there is good news from Lundy, England's only Marine Nature Reserve (see page 151). A recent draft report by conservation scientists shows that there are now three times as many lobsters inside the area's 'no catch zone' compared to other areas where fishing continues.

Many environmentalists, such as the pressure group Greenpeace, propounded such reserves as the way forward. There are now proposals for 17 marine reserves in the North and Baltic Seas, including 85,000 square kilometres in the Dogger Bank area. Linked to meaningful quotas and the well-financed monitored implementation of fishery rules, they offer a glimpse of a sea in which fishermen and fish can both co-exist sustainably.

Thanks to the fecundity of most marine organisms, all we have to do is clean up our act, give them a little peace and quiet and even species heading for extinction can bounce back. The frightening thing is that once a species is gone, it is gone forever – making rebalancing much more difficult, if not impossible.

A future for the sea

Gaze into the crystal ball and you can see another, even more optimistic, vision for the future of the sea. For many environmentalists, its future sustainable redevelopment would put the world's fisheries back in the hands of local fishing communities and all fish and shellfish for the mass market would be from properly-run closed circuit farms that used no chemicals and caused no pollution or eutrophication. The farmed fish would be fed, not on capelin and sand eels (the industrial harvesting of which destroys the base of the marine food web), but on worms or other invertebrates cultured on organic waste.

Gone would be the days of long lining that sentences hundreds of thousands of our sea-birds every year to death by drowning. Gone would be the horrendous by-catch that includes cetaceans thrown back dead into the sea. Then and only then would the whales, dolphins, walruses, seals, sea-lions, sea-birds and local fishers be safe. Along with all the rest of the biodiversity, they would maintain the balance while helping to keep those all important solar-powered sea defences – coral and other reefs – in repair and able to do their all-important jobs as nature's own fish-farms.

With all marine systems back in more natural balance, the life-giving sea could continue to service the biosphere, Gaia-sphere or whatever you want to call it, locking up carbon into long-term storage, producing oxygen and recycling sulphur as slightly acidic rain, as it has done throughout evolutionary time. Sulphur is the element that holds the proteins of all living things together.

PERRAN SANDS AND PENHALE DUNES

MOD/SAC/Bourne for quality leisure time and conservation

A green partnership between a caravan park and the Ministry of Defence may seem somewhat outlandish but the needs of a very special area of land have brought them both together down in the south west of England.

The place is Perran Sands, set in a Special Area of Conservation (SAC) on the astounding coast of Cornwall. Its sandy beaches make for super holidays and its sand dunes make great ranges for the army as well as a fabulous habitat for wildflowers and wildlife. In fact, the dunes surrounding Perran Sands are one of the best habitats in the UK for rare species of plants such as shore dock, early gentian and petalwort.

The commitment of the MOD to conservation is legendary, thanks to their magazine *Sanctuary*, one of the best reads on the subject I know. Bourne Leisure, which owns half the site and 36 other caravan parks across Britain, is following in their mould. Once they got together things really started to buzz.

Since Spring 2002, the Penhale Sands SAC has been managed by a committee that includes all the main landowners along with representation from local statutory, voluntary and business bodies. The results are a credit to all concerned. Much more of the area remains undisturbed, hence animal numbers have gone up – for example, the skylark population has doubled in recent years.

"Partnership is the way forward for the future success of British wildlife," says Bourne Leisure's Christa Sinclair. "As landowners, we have a responsibility to conserve and enhance the wildlife on our parks, but we also have a great opportunity to show our guests what amazing, special places they are and can be."

One of the key decisions the committee has made is to set up a pilot project to employ a ranger. She now helps to promote a greater awareness and appreciation of the site, both within the local community and among the many visitors (including MOD training cadets). She promotes safe and environmentally-aware enjoyment of these important dunes, planning an annual programme of events in the SAC. She also keeps her eye open for good news and for trouble – tackling the latter by working with the appropriate groups. According to Christa, "The ranger has increased enjoyment and appreciation of the dune system amongst our guests and the company's GreenTeam members." Environmental education while on holiday: there's a turn up for the holiday brochures and for the natural history books!

The commitment of all involved in the scheme is obvious. Rather than wait to try and obtain government funding for the project, Bourne Leisure and the MOD were so passionate about getting it started that they decided to take the bull by the horns and share the cost forever.

It was not all plain sailing; a lot of work had to be done to convince all the parties involved that it would be a good idea. Again, Bourne Leisure helped to lead the way, this time by example: by showing the group that similar schemes the company already had up and running in other parks were successes, benefiting both business and wildlife. This gave everybody the confidence to go ahead at Penhale.

Thank goodness they did, because at Penhale Sands we now have a great example of a place where people can come and enjoy a wonderful part of the British landscape and learn about it at the same time. Many holidaying families are taking up the challenge and working together to be able to wear the badge of 'Family Park Ranger'. This is a great scheme run nationwide by Bourne Leisure, to get people interested and involved in conservation. It's something I've personally been involved with: I never thought that I would be asked to help train over 400 Fun Stars, who are part of Bourne Leisure's on-site team of dancers and entertainers, as natural historians, but it is great fun and it's working wonders.

That's not all Bourne Leisure are doing to show their commitment to the environment: members of the local Wildlife Trusts and other conservation groups are invited on free holidays. The only work they have to do is what they like doing best of all – checking out the wildlife, so providing expert proof of just how good the parks are and advice to help make them better.

All this commitment is also helping to balance other books. It has translated into customer satisfaction and repeat bookings, and has also helped the company build strong bridges with the local community from which it draws much of its workforce.

I'm proud to say that this work grew as part of the British Holidays and Home Park Association's Conservation Awards. This scheme is something I have helped champion and it is now almost a decade old.

For further information, please see the Bourne Leisure website at:
www.bourneleisure.co.uk

SAS AND THE NUMBER TWOS

Going through the motions

Giant inflatable 'turds' are not usually bog standard issue for people interested in saving the environment, but then the group who use them, Surfers Against Sewage, is no ordinary group of guys and gals. They are environmentalists in the raw and when they ride the waves on their boards they don't like doing it in raw sewage!

SAS, as they are known, have been campaigning for a clean-up of the seas around the UK since 1990. Their message – that we should not have to swim in our own effluent – has had a profound effect on the government, industry and the general public and has helped bring about changes in how much of Britain's sewage is treated properly. Ever since their group was formed, SAS have argued that simply dumping sewage out at sea through a long pipe isn't treatment. As surfers, the group had first-hand experience of what this actually meant, as they had to swim through the sewage and rubbish that people flushed down their loos. Stomach illnesses and ear infections were just some of the problems they faced as they paddled through the poo, thus they were determined to make the seas and beaches off the UK safer for all swimmers and holidaymakers.

For SAS, the solution is primary, secondary and tertiary treatment, a 'full treatment' process in which sewage is screened and filtered, treated with micro-organisms and then disinfected with either UV-light or microfiltration.

Over the years, they have pushed this message through a whole series of inspired demonstrations and a lot of well-researched campaigning. Thanks in part to their work, companies such as Welsh, Wessex and Yorkshire Water have now all adopted a full treatment policy. Overall, Britain is now on its way to having some of the cleanest beaches and bathing waters in Europe.

Despite this success, there is still a lot of work to be done and SAS are definitely not resting on their laurels, or their surfboards. A new government environment programme for the industry aims to bring in tertiary treatment at 100 additional treatment works in the UK. That means full sewage treatment for a further eight million people. SAS are keeping up the pressure on companies that are dragging their feet and on those who say that this extra treatment does not make sense and will mean extra bills for consumers.

As I write, campaigners from the group dressed as surfing 'cowboys' were at a London water industry meeting calling for the implementation of a full environmental programme for the whole UK water industry. "The water industry has unsuccessfully highlighted the environment as 'the one to cut' to curb bills. In reality, it adds little to bills and provides massive benefits," says Richard Hardy, SAS Campaigns Director. "The industry must start to 'think green' to meet both pending water legislation and customer demands. A full environment programme won't cost the earth and must be delivered before water companies give their shareholders the 'fistful of dollars' they have been receiving year on year."

SAS have calculated that, in the South West Water region, a full environmental improvements programme would contribute less than three pence per day to bills over the 2005-2010 period – £10.95 a year, surely a small price to pay for a safer and cleaner water environment. They also argue that the economic benefits of cleaner beaches are enormous – cleaner beaches bring in more tourists, boosting the local economy. "The coastal and inland water environment must be recognised for the valuable resource it is," says the group. As anyone who has enjoyed a day at one of Britain's newly-clean beaches can testify – they are right.

For further information, please see the SAS website at:
www.sas.org.uk

WHALE-WATCHING

Means business

There are few sights in the portfolio of natural history that are as exciting as watching a pod of whales breaching or a school of dolphin riding off the bow of a boat. The amazing thing is that you do not have to go to the other end of the world to meet the cetaceans face to face. Whale-watching and dolphin-spotting are increasingly popular around the coasts of Scotland – from the Isle of Mull to the Moray Firth, there are lots of opportunities to go to see these marine mammals enjoying themselves. These include minke whales, bottle-nose dolphins and porpoises; animals that live alongside many other amazing sea creatures such as basking sharks and seals.

As anyone who has ever been cetacean-spotting knows, it is one of the best ways of getting people interested in the ocean and passionate about its conservation. The glimpse of some of nature's most fantastic mammals is enough to spark a lifelong interest in even the most jaded of visitors. This is as true in Scotland as it is in, say, Antarctica. In fact, according to recent reports, whales and dolphins are among Scotland's leading wildlife attractions, with hundreds of thousands of tourists making the pilgrimage to see what is in the sea off Scotland's rugged coastline.

This is good news for conservation and it is also good news for the Scottish economy, for in some far-flung areas whale-watching now provides a significant proportion of local income. At a time when traditional sources of income for fishing communities are being lost, this opportunity to diversify into eco-tourism is more vital than ever. Many of the whale-watching companies operating around Scotland are small-scale operations that help supplement the incomes of farmers and fishermen. They attract tourists who then go on to spend more money in B&Bs, cafés and gift shops. It's been calculated that this knock-on effect from whale-watching puts almost £8 million into the economy of west Scotland. How's that for a sustainable harvest?

If you want to see whales or dolphins in Scotland, one of the best areas to start is the Hebrides – the first place I ever saw a killer whale in the wild. What an experience! Mull is the home base to the Hebridean whale and the Dolphin Trust, which pioneered codes of practice and is carrying out a long-term study of the resident populations of bottle-nose dolphins – inquisitive animals that appear to like watching us as much as we like watching them.

Another region in which you are almost guaranteed that thrill of a lifetime is the Moray Firth. Here, boats operate under the Dolphin Space Programme. This is a code of conduct aimed at providing marine wildlife-watching opportunities that do not cause disturbance to the wildlife. This is part of the Moray Firth Conservation Management Scheme, which is designed to protect species such as the bottle-nose dolphin and protect important natural features such as the underwater sandbanks in the area. It's an exciting development that shows how those involved in the whale-watching business are keen not to kill their particular golden goose.

The challenge for Scotland's whale-watching industry is now to step up this kind of regulation to ensure long-term environmental sustainability, while at the same time marketing themselves to as wide a public as possible, so that people think of the Scottish coast as the place to see amazing creatures other than the haggis. With almost 12,000 kilometres of coastline to its name, the potential is huge!

There is no doubt that increasing numbers of cetaceans are enjoying life in British waters and only yesterday did I thrill to the sight of dolphins at play in Plymouth Sound. We can only guess how many Drake saw from his vantage point on Plymouth Hoe and hope that commercial whaling will never be given the go-ahead, especially now we know so much about these sentient creatures.

For further information, please see the website at:
www.greentourism.org.uk/DSP

FISHING WITH A FUTURE

Prawns get the stamp of sustainability

Almost every day seems to bring yet more bad news about fishing and fish stocks in UK waters and indeed around the world. Decades of over-fishing mean that boats, ships and even fleets are being mothballed in an attempt to toe the line of ever more stringent quotas. The sad result is that whole fishing communities now face ever more uncertain economic futures as they, and we as a nation, struggle with the harsh realities of future sustainable supplies of this crucially important part of a healthful diet.

The good news is that the fishing communities themselves are beginning to work on practicable solutions. Amidst the stunning scenery of Loch Torridon, local creelers have got together to make sure that the waters they fish are protected from over-exploitation. It's been a long, hard struggle, but at last they've been successful: the Torridon Creeler Fishery is the first and currently the only one in Scotland to have gained the Marine Stewardship Council's (MSC) standard for well-managed and sustainable fisheries. Only seven fisheries in the world have so far gained this independently-assessed status. The others in the UK are the South West Mackerel Handline Fishery and the Thames Herring Fishery.

If you are like me, you'll love the taste of the seafood that comes out of the Loch. The Torridon creelers catch a kind of small lobster called *Nephrops norvegicus*. Fresh in the restaurants, it goes under a number of different names: langoustines, Dublin Bay prawns, Norway lobster or, locally, just prawns that make your mouth water. Their fight to get the Nephrops fisheries sustainable began in the mid-1990s when local fishermen Kenny Livingstone and John MacGregor decided to try to do something about the effects of over-fishing by trawler fleets in the Loch. They had already seen the area's herring and whitefish stocks crash due to over-exploitation and they did not want to see the same thing happen to their beloved prawns.

After a long, hard struggle, which took them to the highest political level, Kenny and John's work came good in 2001, with the establishment of three fishing zones in the Torridon area: one for creel-only fishing, one for mixed gear fishing and one for trawl fishing only.

John and Kenny now work in a jointly-owned local company called Shieldaig Export Ltd with other creel fishermen. All the boats that work under the creel-only fishery banner have signed a voluntary code of practice, to make sure that they do not damage the ecosystem of the Loch. To do this, they limit the amount of fishing they do and the size of the prawns they catch. The creelers do negligible damage to the seabed and the rest of the marine environment. There is also little impact on other animals, because by-catch in their creels is negligible. And with help from WWF, the fishermen installed escape hatches in their creels. These allow juvenile prawns to escape – vital if the fisheries are to have a long-term future.

Shieldaig Export supplies live prawns to restaurants all over Europe and can get a much better price for their quality product in comparison to the deep-frozen dead seafood produced by many of their competitors. Since the work supports many more people than a trawler-based system, it is win, win, win, both for the local environment and the local economy. Och! Och! The monster of over-fishing has gone from at least part of the loch!

The stamp of approval of the MSC shows just what a good job the guys in Torridon are doing. The MSC's distinctive label is a mark that everyone should look out for at the fish shop as well as in restaurants. More and more products now have the label, so you can buy them safe in the knowledge that they come from a well-managed fishery that has no part in killing their local golden goose. As the Torridon creelers show, it means a future for the sea and for the people whose livelihoods depend on it.

For further information, please see the website at: www.msc.org

LUNDY ISLAND

England's only Marine Nature Reserve so far

Lundy Island lies off the North Devon coast in the waters of the Bristol Channel. In the seas that crash against its rocky shores, cold Atlantic waters mix with warm currents from the Mediterranean. This means that conditions are ideal for an amazing diversity of sea life: an abundance which contains some of England's rarest and most wonderful marine plants and animals including the pink seafan, the sex-changing cuckoo wrasse and the sunset cup coral.

In fact, Lundy and the seas around it are so special that, in 1986, the island was given special protection when it became England's first and only Marine Nature Reserve. Lundy is not just important for what it contains, it is also crucial as a model for protected marine areas that could provide a vital part of any plan to save the UK's seas.

Over the years, the reserve itself has faced many of the problems that affect the rest of Britain's territorial waters. Observations have shown that even in its protected waters, some coral species have declined and some non-commercial species have also become more scarce.

If Lundy faces these challenges, just think what the rest of Britain's waters face. It's clear that the protection and restoration of the marine environment is vital. However, according to English Nature, current government plans for an "experimental programme of multiple benefit marine protected areas" do not go far enough to allow for sufficient recovery of marine habitats and species, let alone the ecosystem as a whole.

To do something about sorting out some of the problems, a radical experiment was hatched and, in January 2003, an area of sea on the east side of Lundy Island was designated as the first statutory No Take Zone (NTZ) for marine nature conservation in the UK. This means that a two-mile area on the sheltered side of the island (where some of the rarest animals and plants can still be found) is out of bounds for fishermen and anglers. English Nature believes it could take up to ten years before the full impact of the No Take Zone can be judged.

English Nature advocates that the UK needs a network of permanent marine protected areas representative of all habitats and that are closed to extractive uses. Lundy has shown how it can be done. Hopefully we will see this pearl in the Bristol Channel become just one link in a necklace of similar sites all around the UK; sites that will provide breeding space for marine animals and plants to re-establish themselves and restock the seas around them.

At **www.english-nature.org.uk**, you can travel around the reserve and experience a virtual tour of the Lundy Reserve, from its cliff tops to its underwater depths.

ABBOTTS HALL

A modern kingdom fit for Canute

It might seem like a strange thing for a conservation group to do but, in October 2002, Essex Wildlife Trust breached the sea-wall that had protected Abbotts Hall Farm on the coast of Essex from the tides for hundreds of years. Far from being a piece of eco-vandalism, this was instead a visionary piece of habitat re-creation on a grand scale. It was also a dyke-breaking attempt to do something about the threats of flood and coastal erosion – problems which, until recently, have just been dealt with by building ever-stronger sea-walls of earth and concrete at enormous cost.

"What we are trying to do is to create a more natural and hence sustainable coastline," says Essex Wildlife Trust's Director, John Hall, who explains that as the salt-water swirled in through the gap in the sea-wall it began to create over 200 acres of salt-marsh out of what had been arable land. "The twice-daily pulses of high tide now spill onto the new salt-marshes which act as a sort of sponge on the edge of the estuary," he says. "This means that, as well as this superb new habitat and cheaper sea defence costs, the new salt-marsh takes the surge off the top of the tide coming up the estuary, thus taking the pressure off the sea defences upstream of us."

This approach to flooding is known as 'coastal realignment' or 'managed retreat' and it is of great importance in places along the Essex coastline: a bit of Britain that is slowly but surely sinking into the sea. It would be all too easy to blame this on so-called global warming caused by the recent burning of fossil fuels but no, the majority of the apparent sea-level rise in the south and east of the UK has its origins back in the heydays of the Ice Age. The thick ice sheets that then covered northern England and Scotland weighed more heavily on the land than the thinner ice sheets further south. They were heavy enough to warp the

Earth's crust, depressing the northern parts of these islands and raising the south.

Thanks to natural global warming, the glaciers have gone and the lands of the north now rejoice as they rise up. The lands of the south are struggling with a real-time sinking feeling or, to put it in scientific terms, Essex is at the wrong end of 'isostatic rebound'. This meant that a bold experiment just had to be carried out. So, hooray for the Essex Wildlife Trust!

To bring the plan to fruition, the Trust worked with organisations such as the Environment Agency, WWF and English Nature. They had to overcome a lot of deep-seated fear of flooding and concern from both the public and the planners. "Many people thought of it as giving up a piece of England," says John, who explains that they had to jump through many planning hoops for over two years before getting the green light. Now, people are starting to realise that far from losing a bit of the country, Essex has actually gained a valuable and rare piece of habitat that is an important part of local flood protection. "The salt-marsh is doing very well," explains John. "As well as the colonisation by plants, invertebrates and birds such as widgeon, teal and redshank, a tremendous number of fish have started to use the site. We've had 14 species, including many thousands of sea bass and blackwater herring. They come in because the site is a good nursery area, rich in food. The fish then bring in other birds, such as little egret, heron, grebes and diving ducks."

Most people in the region are now very positive about the project. Oystermen who were worried about their livelihoods see the new salt-marshes as food for their oysters. The main people still unsure are the arable farmers who appear to be on the losing end of an ever-shrinking wicket. Here, the Essex Wildlife Trust are trying something really novel – they are experimenting with high-value marsh crops such as glasswort, seakale and even asparagus to show that marshes do not mean that farming has to stop. The Trust is grazing hardy sheep on the upper marshes to produce a high grade premium salt-marsh lamb and it is also continuing to cultivate most of the farm with arable crops to look at the profitability of the whole farm unit.

From a wildlife point of view, however, it is the marshes themselves that are so important. The habitat that has been created is vital for this part of the world. Essex estuaries have lost up to 60% of their salt-marshes due to other less visionary methods of protecting the coast from the effects of isostatic rebound, while over 90% of its coastal grazing marshes have been lost to arable land and development, all dependent on sea-walls, expensive to build and more expensive to maintain. Every year around 100 hectares of salt-marsh is lost in the south and east of England. This makes Abbotts Hall farm, which sits on the Blackwater Estuary, an internationally important area for wildlife, especially significant.

What's been done at Abbotts Hall, which is currently the largest managed retreat project in Europe, could now be used as a model for coastal management in many other places in the UK. There are now plans for an even bigger project in Wallasea in south Essex. This will use data from Abbotts Hall and a computer estuary model that was developed as part of the Abbotts Hall project. What is clear is that walls are not a long-term solution on every section of the coast; they merely push the problem onto someone else's patch. Abbotts Hall shows that, by working with nature and the sea, we can make gains for wildlife and peace of mind for those who live along the coast.

For further information, please see the website at:
www.essexwt.org.uk

Chapter 7

DOWN ON THE FARM

Lark Rise Farm in Cambridgeshire is one oasis where we can still appreciate the countryside as it used to be. Its fields and brooks teem with wildlife such as brown hare and otter; cowslip, cornflower and corncockle nod alongside the crops; barn owls nest in its barns and unkempt about its hedgerows blows the unofficial English rose. This is a working, profitable farm in which the ghost of Rupert Brooke would feel at home. Run by a visionary group called the Countryside Restoration Trust, it shows how farming and conservation can and must go hand-in-hand.

The work of the Trust (see page 172) is one inspiring answer to a question that is at the heart of nature conservation in the UK: is there a future for the rest of Britain's lowland farmlands?

Even if you've never set foot outside the M25, you have used and enjoyed lowland Britain. In fact, every time you go into your local supermarket and buy a trolley of food you will, more likely than not, have bought something grown on a UK farm. Farmland takes up about two-thirds of the UK countryside and, believe it or not, still supplies over 60% of all the indigenous food we eat – not bad going for a small, densely-populated island.

Unfortunately, getting all this food into the nation's grocery stores and onto the nation's tables has come at a price. Martin Doughty, head of English Nature, was a speaker at the RSA Balance of Nature conference. "Unimproved hay meadows have declined by 97%, between the 1930s and the 1980s, and the decline continues at 2 to 10% per annum," he said. With the loss of these hay meadows has come the wholesale loss of flowers. No flowers, no nectar; no nectar, no insects; no insects, no skylarks; no skylarks, no kestrels. It's a vicious cycle, driven by habitat destruction caused by a change in the way the land is managed. Indeed, the loss of hay meadows and other vital habitats such as hedgerows, woodlands and fens has led to the decline and loss of many species from large areas, turning much of Britain's four million hectares of lowland farms into wildflower, and hence wildlife, deserts.

Modern, industrialised farming has also caused massive amounts of water use, many once-vibrant trout-streams have dried up due to ground water abstraction, and water and soil pollution from pesticide and fertiliser leakage have compounded the problem. Experts such as Jules Pretty from the University of Essex calculate a cost of around £135 million each year to remove such pollutants from drinking water – a cost paid for by water consumers, not by the polluters.

The impact of the CAP

The main reasons for these problems are well known and were outlined by Tim Nevard at the conference. The Common Agriculture Policy (or CAP), born out of the desire to make Europe self-sufficient in food, promoted ever-increasing levels of production through subsidies. These subsidies, linked with new technologies and methods of farming and driven by the demands of the supermarket giants for more reliable supplies of ever-cheaper food, have pushed farming in one direction: bigger and more mechanised farms, using vast amounts of chemicals to grow mono-culture crops. Sadly, a recipe for a lot of food, but not for much wildlife.

This mechanisation and corporatisation of farming has not helped the population of rural Britain either; farming numbers fell by almost half between 1977 and 1993. Indeed, thanks to this farming revolution, there has been an ongoing loss of farmers and farmworkers from the countryside. Small farms have disappeared, and fast – on average 4,000 have been driven out of business every year for the past 50 years, with devastating results for many rural economies.

The Countryside Restoration Trust is showing what can be done on a small scale, but the question still remains: can we reconcile our desire for cheap food with a countryside replete with all the wildlife that should be there? Such questions about the future of the working countryside were at the heart of the challenge laid down by HRH Prince Philip at the RSA conference.

The good news is that important answers are being sought by a growing number of forward-thinking farmers, food producers and retailers the length and breadth of Britain. And – according to what they are finding and putting into practice – the answer appears to be a 'yes'. There are, of course, a few 'buts' attached.

Rewarding 'good' agriculture

Along with the stalwarts of the organic movement – such as the Henry Doubleday Research Association and the Soil Association – the Farming and Wildlife Advisory Group (FWAG) have been at the forefront of environmentally-sensitive agriculture for over 25 years. The FWAG encourage farmers to implement a whole host of relatively simple – but effective – ways to encourage wildlife down on the farm: from wildlife-sensitive hedge-trimming, to creating buffer zones around fields.

Each year, the FWAG present the Silver Lapwing Award to the farm that is best managed to encourage wildlife and enrich the countryside while being farmed on a strictly commercial basis. The rich harvest of annual entries points to the fact that there are many farmers who are already working tirelessly to that end. These farmers draw on their (and their colleagues') skills as agronomists, gamekeepers, ecologists and natural history buffs to create farms in good heart and more in balance with nature.

The winner of the Silver Lapwing Award in 2003 was Partridge Hill Farm near Doncaster. The work carried out by this farm (see page 175) speaks volumes for what can be achieved: 5 acres of conservation headlands, 8,500 metres of field margins and 6.5 acres of wild bird mixes have been introduced over the farm. The resulting mosaic of habitats encourages a variety of species, including no fewer than 75 different types of birds – among them linnet, bullfinch, song thrush and lapwing, all back down on the farm.

The FWAG are not alone and there are many, many groups – including the national network of Wildlife Trusts and the RSPB – who work with farmers to help them wade through all the paperwork to make the most of grants that pay them to improve the environmental performance of their farms. One Lincolnshire farmer whom I know well even worked out the best way to keep us supplied with a reliable source of spuds without cashing in the chips for the environment (see page 177).

Farmers are finding many benefits from going green. For example, one in North Yorkshire has proved that high-tech integrated crop management uses up to one-third less farm chemicals and so increases his profit, while helping to ensure that the farm buzzes with biodiversity once again.

In the old days, farmers did it out of necessity. With no subsidies, they couldn't afford to chuck expensive lime and fertilisers where they couldn't produce results. They knew their land and were high-precision farmers putting fertilisers only on the best bits and certainly not into the rivers. Their modern day eco-efficient counterparts are replete with computers and satellites that do it all from the air-conditioned cab of a tractor that ploughs and sprays only the most productive bits of the land, managing the other bits for wildflowers and wildlife. Little or nothing goes to waste and young farmers love all the gadgets of technology transfer.

A lot of this work is, of course, financed by the government, which runs a number of 'agri-environment' schemes to help farmers

A Bellamy nature masterclass

Heather moorland – one of the world's rarest habitats (page 48)

Stanage Edge and ring ouzel (page 61)

Joe Relph and his Herdwick sheep (page 63)

A trout-stream – lifeblood of a living landscape

"What's all the fuss about?"

"Silver satanic windmills" – and not a power station saved

The River Thames is now the cleanest river flowing through any capital city in Europe

An example of Conservation Grade farming (pages 179 and 182)

The author and friends at one of Bourne Leisure's caravan parks
(page 193)

Far Grange Park (page 213)

The perception that hunting mammals with dogs is cruel conflicts with the belief that it is the least cruel means of controlling pests or harvesting game

*The red squirrel – fighting back with a little help from its friends
(page 92)*

Jellied eels: a dish of the past? (page 127)

Surfers say "no" to sewage (page 144)

Abbotts Hall Farm (page 153)

to take environmental issues 'on board'. These include the latest Environmental Stewardship 'Entry' and 'Higher' Level Schemes and the Environmentally-Sensitive Areas (ESA) scheme. Boring acronyms they may be, but they hold an important part of the answer.

Thanks to such schemes – and to the work of organisations like the FWAG – a significant number of farmers now manage, protect and help to restore those all-important wetlands, hedgerows and wildflower meadows across the UK. However, these examples of best practice, as they stand, are simply not widespread enough or, in many instances, far-reaching enough to bring about a significant increase in wildlife across large sections of Britain's lowlands. They are certainly not enough to undo the environmental devastation of the second half of the twentieth century, but they represent an important series of steps in the right direction.

Light at the end of the agricultural tunnel?

Two encouraging recent developments could change this state of affairs for the better. The first light at the end of the tunnel is the latest round of reforms to the Common Agricultural Policy. In the face of mounting pressure from environmentalists, farmers and the public, in June 2003, EU farm ministers adopted a fundamental reform of the CAP, which will bring in a single farm payment for EU farmers that is not dependent on production. This payment will instead be linked to requirements to keep farmland in good agricultural and environmental condition.

These proposals – which are being rolled out during 2004 and 2005 – have been greeted by many as a very positive move that could remove the main driving force that encourages farmers to farm as much of their land as possible in the most intensive way. Instead, the new subsidies should encourage more farmers to switch to less intensive methods of farming and take full advantage of the many agri-environment schemes run by the government.

One of the main things wrong with the old-style subsidies was that they did not do enough to encourage good management of any farmland taken out of production – so-called 'set aside' areas. The new CAP reforms could provide the incentive for farmers to grow biodiversity as well as they can grow their mainstay crops.

Exactly what can be achieved has been shown by the Manor Farm project which, thanks to farmer Richard Brown and visionary agronomist Marek Nowakowski, has proved that it can be done (see page 179).

Overall, the CAP reforms should help remove one of the most significant barriers in the way of environmentally-sensitive farming in the UK. However, many doubt that even these reforms will be enough to bring about a massive improvement in the fortunes of Britain's wildlife. For this, they argue, you need nothing less than a sea-change, dare I say a managed advance, in the way food production – and the countryside – is thought about by both the public and the farming community.

Buying biodiversity in the shops

One mechanism that may bring about a true green revolution in UK farming is, at first sight, an unlikely one. After all, it has been blamed for many of farming's environmental woes. Be that as it may, the market and consumer demand is now being used by an increasing number of farmers to deliver a way of farming with the environment not just in mind, but at the heart of things.

In November 2003, the value of organic produce (accredited by organisations such as the Soil Association) bought in the UK's shops topped the one billion pound mark for the first time. Admittedly, this otherwise impressive figure is a drop in the ocean in the UK's £100 billion plus food sector. Be that as it may, it has shown that there is demand for food produced in a more environmentally-friendly way, pointing the way for other farmers to capitalise on the demand to make a more environmentally-friendly living.

The organic movement, led by groups such as Henry Doubleday, the Soil Association and, of course, the Prince of Wales, has done Trojan work and shows that it is possible to produce good healthful food in abundance with less harmful inputs. However, that's not to say that organic farming is the way all British farming will, or should, go – there are other ways that bring many, if not all, of the benefits and fewer of the drawbacks of a total chemical ban down in the barn; ways that help farmers to better profits while they bring more of their farmland back into good heart. All are much better than threatening the viability of more farms by applying the 'polluter pays' principle to clean up any mess.

One good example of this is the LEAF marque. This is an accreditation scheme that recognises high standards of environmental responsibility on farms. Another 'eco' farming standard, which more people are getting to know about, is 'Conservation Grade' farming. Farmers who sign up for this scheme make a commitment to various environmental projects on their farms, such as the promotion of 'in-field' biodiversity (see page 182). This isn't organic, but it is a comprehensive 'whole-farm' approach to nature conservation.

Most importantly, 'Conservation Grade' farming, like the LEAF Marque, is consumer-driven. It is already a key selling point for millions of 'Frusli' bars that also boast they contain no additives. Similarly, all the cereals in the Jordans 'Country Crisp' range are sourced from Conservation Grade farms.

What makes these schemes so important is that the consumer can trust them. An audited production stream and a reliable label means that any shopper can have faith in the product and the claims it is making. So, when they select it from the shelves, they are making an informed choice about helping Britain's wildlife.

Partnerships for the countryside

New partnerships between farmers and food producers are emerging all across the UK food and agriculture sector. In the 2003 Radio 4 Food and Farming Awards, Yeo Valley Foods – famous for their yoghurts – won a prize for their work producing food which supports environmentally-sensitive farming. The company explained that one recent project involved working with British sugar producers to help them convert to organic agriculture. Yeo Valley Foods placed a guaranteed order, the sweetener that helped to persuade their potential suppliers they needed to go down the organic track.

These partnerships between farmers, producers and ultimately consumers are vital, since they funnel more money to those food producers who are heading in the right direction.

To use the economist and environmentalist Tim Nevard's words, "In these days, farmers and small farmers in particular just do not have the economic ability to be overtly 'friendly' towards anybody other than their bank managers. To be able to follow their natural inclination and manage their land back into good heart is a luxury that most cannot afford, unless they are paid to do so."

Carrots, not the sticks of 'polluter pays' litigation, are surely the best way ahead. Such schemes, of course, need the support of all concerned and this fact has already produced a number of difficult challenges for farmers who want to farm in a greener way. Some supermarkets are pressuring their organic suppliers to keep prices low, which has meant that the economics no longer make much sense and some go to the wall.

The big boys can, of course, switch to cheaper supplies from abroad. The good news is that our farmers have found a way of getting round this problem – to cut out all the middle-people. Here lies one of the most exciting marketing developments of recent years – the rise of farmers' markets, where producer and consumer once again meet face to face.

There are, of course, some charlatans even in this business, but research by the NFU has shown that these markets, where producers sell directly to consumers, now earn cash-strapped farmers a total of £166 million a year. What is even more exciting, their numbers more than doubled in the two years to 2004, from 200 to 450.

Real farmers have always enjoyed the challenge and the camaraderie of the local market and so have their customers. Each one is a focal point in local rural life. Now they are making a comeback, part of a new social hormone that is rebinding farmer and consumer – dare I say town and country – back together.

A darker side of this whole matter is that some big players appear to be targeting the many thousands of organic farms in countries that are queuing up to join the Common Market and persuading them to go down what is essentially the old CAP way, to supply our home market: bad news for the biodiversity of a wider Europe and for the number of miles the food, including live animals, have to travel.

Fewer food miles

This leads neatly on to another attraction of 'farmers' markets', which by their 'local' nature reduce another major environmentally-unfriendly aspect of today's modern food business, namely food miles. Food miles are the distance that food has to travel to get from field to spoon and fork. The worst offenders are supermarkets that truck home-grown food from one end of the country to a central distribution centre, only to send it back again for sale in the shop (of course, imported food takes this particular ball game to another level).

So, what is the future for food production and wildlife here in Britain? Will a combination of 'better' subsidies, agri-environment schemes, eco-labels and farmers' markets put both the ecology and the economy of the countryside back on its feet? Will we see local brands with packaging that illustrates the portfolio of wildlife present on the farms it came from or even with microchips attached to sing the consumer the morning chorus recorded down on that particular farm? And, perhaps most importantly, what is it all going to cost us at the check-out?

This last question is not only important in terms of the weekly shopping bill, it's also vital because of the deeper issues it raises and the challenges it poses.

First, let's take a look at the cost of 'normal' intensively-farmed food and compare it to organic food, thought by many to be the cream of the crop when it comes to encouraging wildlife down on the farm. At first glance, it may look like no contest – the non-organic food is much cheaper.

But stop to consider that, apart from the bill for the food, you already pay the subsidies and the cost of cleaning up any damage that may have been caused by the farming that produced it. As we have already seen, the bill for cleaning up the pesticide residue costs the tax-payer around £135 million each year, not including the cost to the NHS and to business for sick leave caused by any illness that pollution and chemical residues may have produced.

Many also argue that food produced on less intensive farms is usually tastier, more nutritious and involves less cruelty to animals. There are, of course, goodies and baddies on both sides, but there is no getting away from the fact that food produced the less intensive way often includes interesting and delicious local cheeses, yoghurts, apples and other fruits alongside free-range fish, fowl and meat.

Add into this equation the fact that organic food has, until now, often got fewer subsidies than 'conventional' farming and all of a sudden organic food doesn't seem to be that much more expensive. What is more, if the subsidies change in the right way, the differences could be slashed. Already, if you shop around (especially at a farmers' market) you can avoid highly-processed foodstuffs or save yourself

166

money by buying the raw materials and doing it yourself. Given the current high viewing figures for cookery shows and the sale of cookery books, naked or hardback, this should already be happening on a massive scale! Another good tip is to join the Women's Institute and learn to pluck a pheasant, gut a fish and even jug a hare (once they become more numerous).

The future of farming?

The billion dollar question is what is going to happen? British farming is faced by increasing competition from abroad, where good farmland is less scarce, labour is cheaper and hence prices are lower. It may sound like the answer to our greenest prayers but if British farming was wound down who would manage the land, keeping alive the mosaic of different habitats that give the British countryside its character and biodiversity?

The good news is that more and more people are cottoning on to the fact that the best way to save the country's wildlife is to vote with their willow shopping baskets, well-laced with first-hand information as to how the countryside works. That is why more and more farmers are looking to embrace environmentally-friendly farming, complete with gamekeepers and ghillies – helped along the way by 'good' subsidies that allow them to manage their land, with conservation of wildlife an added earner.

To feed both fast and slow foodies in Britain, be they resident or visitors, requires a massive effort. Lest we forget, chickens, ducks, turkeys, cattle and every other domesticated animal we choose to eat or have to kill, in the process of feeding ourselves and our families, do deserve due care and attention. All should be treated with the dignity they deserve: as stress-free a life as possible, no long journeys to an abattoir and a short, sharp, shock that kills instantly. The same is true of all game-birds and animals; there must be no difference in their treatment, for there is none in the ethic of their utility to humankind.

167

Even those who eschew the consumption of flesh must take into account that even the best organic farms always have to safeguard against attack by animals and birds, let alone insects.

This reconnection between the consumer and the countryside – between rural and urban Britain – is what is needed to bring balance back to the farms of lowland Britain. If it happens, then shoppers will not only be able to purchase good, more natural food, but also to be part of a good, more balanced landscape with less downstream environmental costs: farming with real added value.

THE SHOOTING BOX

If you want to find out the impact that farming and other forms of land management have on our countryside, then take a look at the history of the field sports. Details of game shot on the country's sporting estates have been recorded in ledgers or game books for many years, sometimes for more than a century. These records provide a window on how game management has affected the balance of wildlife in the countryside.

This archive covers game such as grouse, grey partridge, geese, duck, roe and red deer along with all non-native animal introductions like pheasants and rabbits. (Rabbits with their unique reproductive capabilities have, of course, become such a pest that they have to be kept under control in order to keep farmers in business. However, until the advent of myxomatosis, they formed an important part of Britain's diet.) But that's not the only information that game books provide; some records contain details of predators such as foxes, crows and mink and a host of other smaller birds and animals.

This invaluable historical record has been used by Dr Stephen Tapper of the Game Conservancy to find out how gamekeeping affects the ecology of areas where shooting has taken place. According to Stephen, study of these historical records proves that hunting and shooting have helped shape the British countryside over the past 200 years – especially its woodlands and its moors. The New Forest and Cranborne Chase are just two examples of landscapes that were created for hunting and which are now recognised as National Parks and Areas of Outstanding Natural Beauty. Less well known is the fact that many Victorian and Edwardian country estates were acquired and managed for their sporting interest – hunting in some areas, shooting in others. In fact, the study of archives and maps proves that many of the small woods, spinneys and copses that feature in English Nature's descriptions of the character of their 'Natural Areas' owe their existence to hunting and shooting.

Today, hunting and shooting continue to play a significant part in keeping the countryside as we expect it to be. Pheasants make up the largest percentage of the game-bag in the lowlands of Britain and many landowners work hard to improve their land for holding both wild and reared birds by planting woods, retaining hedges and trying to adopt wildlife-friendly techniques on the farmland that they manage. All this in the teeth of the newer plagues of grey squirrel, sika, muntjac, mink and feral cats, dogs and even pigs. Some would include the plague of what are now called 'battery pheasant' shoots where numbers shot not quality shooting rules the roost, driving down both the name and the value of the game.

Sadly, things are not all rosy; after reviewing the records from the Edwardian era to the present day, Stephen found that, in shoots across the country, the majority of wild game are declining and many of the predatory species increasing. This problem is due to many factors: two world wars took many able countrymen away to foreign fields and took their toll on home front countryside management. Digging for victory may have helped us win one war but it paved the way for the inanities of the Common Agricultural Policy, a war on the Earth that rages to this day. Add to that the effect of all those plagues of introduced animals, which added to the escalating costs of estate management. One further nail in the coffin was the dream of the *nouveau riche*, who invested in their own personal shooting estates without weighing up the real cost of sustainable management. All this helped get parts of our countryside into the sad state they are in today.

What then is the best response to this problem? Fortunately, all is not lost and there is still a noble band of around 5,500 gamekeepers hard at work doing what they have been apprenticed to do: look after game by maintaining balance in the countryside. However, the future of Britain's gamekeepers is far from certain. "Unless sportsmen can shoot the game they cherish, there will be no-one to pay their wages and hence no-one to maintain the living balance. Landowners will then lack much more than the motivation to conserve and manage game birds and the landscape in which they are nurtured," says Stephen. "They will lose heart; turning away from wild game management and instead towards plans for a new golf course, a housing estate, a theme park or a wind factory on their still-rural acres."

This means that, if nothing is done, a valuable conservation resource will vanish from the British countryside. The answer to this problem is to realise that the practice of good gamekeeping is at the heart of the conservation of our countryside and that it does not have to involve the wholesale slaughter of predators. From the game point of view, the object of countryside management is to reduce predation, it is not to do away with natural predators. The majority of gamekeepers know this and use their skills to the benefit of the environment. In fact, there are moves afoot to slowly but surely reintroduce some, if not all, of the native animals – including predators – that have been sent to the wall of local extinction.

For further information, please see the website at: www.gct.org.uk

COUNTRYSIDE RESTORATION TRUST (CRT)

Buying farms for conservation

Everyone can have a vision of 'saving the countryside', but it takes a special type of dedication to turn it into reality, like that of the vision that has become the Countryside Restoration Trust, started in 1993 when it owned just 20 acres of land at Lark Rise Farm in Cambridgeshire. Many doubters said that what it was setting out to do was old-fashioned, inefficient and would not work. However, from this small beginning, the energy and determination of Trust members and volunteers has seen the CRT wage an ever more successful war against the spectre of intensive farming as the only way ahead.

Today, Lark Rise Farm has grown to 400 acres of profitable, habitat-rich arable farmland. Other farms have also been added to the dream, including 20 acres of semi-ancient woodland and a similar area of pastoral farmland in West Yorkshire. The Trust also own Awnells Farm, a beautiful 220-acre grassland farm situated in rural Herefordshire, while its most recent purchase is Turnastone Court, a gem of a farm located in Herefordshire's renowned and beautiful Golden Valley, where the development of a proposed wind farm has been stopped.

Here they have saved 400-year-old hay meadows and pastureland, rich in species, from almost certain destruction. In fact, if the Trust had not bought the property, these meadows would have been turned over to intensive potato growing.

In all, the Trust now owns and manages about 850 acres of farmland and over 40 acres of woodland and productive orchards.

The CRT's aim is to purchase land which has been intensively farmed and restore it through sensitive and sympathetic farming

172

practices, which include the rehabilitation of landscape and habitat for wildlife. From the early days, the CRT has gained over 5,000 'Friends' and raised in excess of £2 million, which has been used in the purchase of land.

The group's approach, which builds on the passion and convictions of the farmers and volunteers it works with, is perhaps best shown at Lark's Rise. Here, thanks to sensitive farming methods such as spring drilling and under-sowing, the creation of grass margins, wildlife strips, headlands, beetle banks and sensible set-aside management, wildlife has returned in abundance. No wonder they boast about the numbers of skylarks rising above their fields. Their singing is a song of success because Lark's Rise has one of the highest densities of skylarks in Cambridgeshire, along with several other breeding birds that are considered rare elsewhere, such as barn owls and grey partridges.

"From the start it was decided that Lark Rise should not go organic. It lies in the heart of prairie-farming land and one of the initial aims was to influence the Barley-Barons," explains Robin Page, CRT's founder and Chairman. "It was felt that if Lark Rise was organic, the mindset of the farming establishment would immediately place it on the eccentric fringe. We wanted Lark Rise's neighbours to see good crops produced in a way they could recognise, but with various environmental add-ons that they might find attractive."

According to Robin, the main barrier stopping other farmers from copying what the Trust is doing comes from the farming establishment itself. "There appears to be much pressure to be seen as a 'modern', 'efficient', 'progressive' farmer," he says. "As a result, some farmers believe that 'neatness' is a prerequisite sign of 'efficiency'. They are wrong, of course, but as a result they can be reluctant to have wilder unkempt ditches and hedges and the idea of grass margins and beetle banks seems to be totally beyond them."

To spread the message that wildlife and profitable farming can go together, the CRT aims to establish a network of Trust farms throughout the country as a focus of inspiration, education and good food. A practical demonstration for farmers, decision makers and the public of one way ahead for farming in Britain. It's an exciting vision which has already been proved to work down on Lark Rise Farm.

For further information, please see the CRT website at:
www.crtbarton.org.uk

PARTRIDGE HILL FARM

Award-winners show the way forward

Lapwings were once a common sight in the British countryside. At last, they are starting to make a comeback. This is in part thanks to the work of farmers such as Tim Paxman and Chris Goodall, who won the 2003 Farmcare FWAG Silver Lapwing Award. Tim and Chris manage Partridge Hill, in Yorkshire.

Their approach at Partidge Hill is very pragmatic: "We have taken areas of poor land and we have looked at ways of obtaining grants to convert it for the benefit of wildlife," says Chris, who has, for example, used the government's Woodland Grant Scheme and Farm Woodland Premium Scheme to develop and maintain the farm's woodlands. Over 10,000 new trees and hedgerow plants have been established. Crucially, Chris feels that the environmental work at Partridge Hill has increased the profitability of the farm and he sees the current CAP reforms as an opportunity for more farmers to follow his lead.

"It's been a process of learning as we go," says Chris, who is particularly pleased with the experimental 220-metre oak hedge they have planted. The hedge has a six metre nectar-rich grass margin next to it, as well as conservation headlands.

According to FWAG, Tim and Chris won their award against stiff competition but got the prize because they enriched the countryside at Partridge Hill while farming on a strictly commercial basis. "The outstanding conservation work at Partridge Hill Farm is an example of what can be achieved with passion, insight and careful planning," said James Money-Kyrle, Chief Executive of FWAG. "The future of farming in the UK depends on combining profitability with a sensitive and imaginative contribution to the environment. Tim Paxman and Chris Goodall have given us an outstanding model of farming and nature in balance."

Partridge Hill is a 330-acre, predominantly arable farm. Sheep and pigs are reared and crops include wheat, barley, oil-seed rape, beans, peas and sugar-beet. In the 20 years that they have been farming Partridge Hill, Chris and Tim have made many environmental improvements, particularly the management and creation of natural wildlife habitats such as ponds, small plantations and hedgerows. Across the farm, agrochemicals are used sparingly. Indeed, the farmers have found that 'good' insects from their network of hedgerows and field margins, allied to a modest average field size, make many chemicals unnecessary. Bees kept on the farm take advantage of the diverse cropping and flora, and contribute to enhanced yields of beans and rape.

"Whether farmers like it or not, politicians and the electorate are going to push farming down the conservation route," says Tim. "Personally, I am quite happy with that. If we provide what the public want then it is going to help us when it comes to marketing our produce. If conservation is carefully thought through, then it doesn't have to conflict with profitability."

For further information, please see the FWAG website at:
www.fwag.org.uk

VINE HOUSE FARM

Practical conservation on the fens

If you have eaten chips or crisps recently, some of them will have come from the fens. They may have even come from the fields of Vine House Farm. Full of birds and other animals, Vine House Farm is an ongoing experiment into how big and small changes in the way that farming is carried out can have a profound impact on the quantity and variety of wildlife that agricultural land can sustain. Not only that but the farmer, Nicholas Watts, also grows birdseed commercially, so that others can join him in the fight to turn up the repertoire and volume of bird song.

Nicholas, winner of lots of conservation awards, has spent many years of trial and error to find out how best to boost the biodiversity of Vine House Farm, where he grows large crops of potatoes organically. Despite his organic ticket (which covers about 20% of his farm) and his credentials as a lifelong natural historian, he found that the wildlife on his farm could still do with an extra helping hand.

Planting clover to add fertility to his fields is a vital part of his approach. However, management of his clover crop was carried out using a vicious machine aptly called a flail mower. This shoots stones and twigs back into hedges, destroying any remaining nests and also killing immature insects and grubs which are the breeding stock for next year.

Nicholas found that, by using a different machine – a pasture topper – sparingly and not during the periods when birds are looking after their broods in the clover, it was possible to dramatically improve the number of birds breeding on his farm. "Most nests do survive under this mower, while none would survive under the flail mower. We now have over 20 pairs of nesting whitethroats," he says proudly.

All over the farm there is evidence of Nicholas' commitment to the environment. He has left redundant dykes in place because they are a valuable habitat for wildlife, created over 25 kilometres of wide field margins, planted the right wildflowers, dug ponds and planted and managed hedges and woodland to provide places for birds to nest and food for them to eat.

At Vine House Farm, set-aside land is not simply left fallow, instead crops (such as sunflowers) are planted for the birds to harvest. Nesting sites for owls have been made by re-roofing redundant farm buildings and by putting up nesting boxes.

Nicholas has seen dramatic increases in bird populations compared to the national average. For example, the owl population has increased by 300% in the last 15 years, the reed bunting population has doubled and reed warblers are doing well. "The reed warblers are doing well because I persuaded the local drainage board to mow our drains once a year. One of the reasons I decided to go organic was because I had recorded such a large reduction in breeding birds on my farm," Nicholas explains. "I am pleased to say that bird populations are increasing and I am enjoying the challenge of organic crops."

Ventures such as Nicholas' could allow all farms with shared boundaries to also share the pleasure and the profit at this, the cutting edge of conservation. Nicholas is just one of a growing band of farmers who are proving that, when it comes to wetlands, boundaries or even whole farm systems, anything is possible. All you need to do is give Mother Nature a little bit of help and the farmer a helping hand along the way to making a truly sustainable living.

For further information, please see the Vine House Farm website at: www.vinehousefarmbirdfoods.co.uk

MANOR FARM AND THE BUZZ PROJECT

A farm-sized biodiversity experiment

If British farmers are so good at growing crops like wheat, barley and oil-seed rape, then they must be able to grow biodiversity, argues agronomist Marek Nowakowski. To find out whether he is right, Marek has teamed up with Farmer Brown (Richard to his friends), at Manor Farm in North Yorkshire. So far, the answer has been 'yes'; in fact results have been so good they have surprised everyone who has seen them. They have proved that creating high quality habitats for wildlife can actually contribute to the profitability of commercial farms.

Now home to the Farmed Environment Company (FEC), Manor Farm is a modern, professionally-managed arable enterprise. The whole team is committed to increasing farmland biodiversity through innovative research and best practice. How do they do it? They create new habitats from the least profitable areas on the farm.

Herb-rich seed mixtures have been planted in field margins, corners and in the areas under trees and pylons. Over three kilometres of new hedgerows have gone in. These are cut less frequently and provide birds with safer nesting sites, more insects for their chicks and autumn berries. In fact, there are plenty of berries to go round; enough to allow the farm to produce sloe gin and sloe chocolate from this hedgerow larder to make a profitable addition to farm income.

This is not an organic farm; chemicals are used, even, on occasions, specially-selected weedkillers that remove weeds, so ensuring the rapid establishment of wild seed mixtures – opening ever more butterfly bars. The Manor Farm approach is all about finding the right answers to improve business and the environment, then putting them into practice. Often, the solutions are surprisingly obvious. "We found that we could bring birds back simply by feeding them and giving them a place to live," says Marek, "so we have provided food and nesting boxes."

That's the birds, what about the bees? Many of Britain's 19 bumble-bee species have suffered serious decline over recent decades. This is bad news because they provide an essential pollination service for many crops and wildflowers. "The countryside is short of the pollen that nectar bees and other insects need," explains Marek, "so we grew the right flowers that produce them in abundance."

To see how things are doing, the whole of Manor Farm is monitored every year to find out exactly how biodiversity has changed. The results are impressive.

Overall, wildlife has increased by about a factor of five. Bird numbers are up, including sharp increases in the numbers of chaffinch and tree sparrow. Many mammals have made their comeback on the farm and breeding is impressive enough to help more hawks and owls be 'to the manor born'. The numbers and varieties of butterflies have increased alongside those of other creepy-crawlies. In fact, the farm now has all the butterfly species possible in this part of Yorkshire.

So what does all this mean for other farmers? According to the Manor Farm team, simply stopping the cropping of poorer areas for the benefit of nature conservation is meaningless unless the quality of the habitat that is produced is high. Manor Farm shows how to create the high-quality habitat wildlife enjoys.

But what about cost? Well, because the least profitable land is taken, and in some cases the alternative land uses can attract grants, the impact of growing wildlife habitats is minimised or can even be profitable. Add to this the fact that using the Manor Farm approach significantly cuts the use of costly agricultural chemicals and suddenly the work makes real economic sense.

What is perhaps most exciting about Manor Farm is that the current reforms of the CAP look set to make such positive work much more profitable and hence more attractive.

"At the moment, subsidies paid to farmers are food-production linked," says Marek. "I believe that the CAP reforms are an opportunity to reward farmers for providing quality habitats for nature. We sit on the edge of the single biggest opportunity to halt the decline of farmland biodiversity." Our wildlife can only hope he's right.

There is no holding the FEC down: an even more ambitious scheme is already underway. The Buzz Project is a five-year research initiative being run on six arable farms in locations ranging from Essex to North Yorkshire. This network of sites forms the basis of training packages which help farmers to learn the new environmental skills that make positive environmental change happen fast.

Already, the results from the Buzz Project are very encouraging, with species counts increasing as dramatically as at Manor Farm – all in the first ten months from sowing.

For further information, please see the Manor Farm and Buzz Project web pages at: www.f-e-c.co.uk

YOUNG BILL JORDAN HAS A FARM

Good news from your cereal bar

When you enjoy one of the wide range of Jordans snack or breakfast products, such as Frusli bars, you can do it safe in the knowledge that the cereals it contains have been grown in a way that enhances wildlife down on the farm.

Jordans is one of the leading examples of a company that is promoting and supporting environmentally-friendly farming through its products and its advertising. It is a family business based in Biggleswade. Its products also bear the reassurance that, while other processed food may contain some artificial additives, theirs contains none. Sales are substantial – enough Fruesli bars to wrap around the world four and a half times each year.

This is really good news for the environment because all the cereals in Jordans' products are grown in the UK to organic standards, or to those of the Guild of Conservation Grade Producers. Conservation Grade is an independently-audited sustainable farming system, which focuses on the environment and has been proven to increase wildlife on farms fivefold, whilst maintaining farm profits.

"Conservation Grade underpins the Jordans brand and helps farmers get their land back into more natural working order," explains Bill Jordan, their Managing Director, who feels that the scheme represents a win-win situation for both business and wildlife.

Jordans have been with the Guild since 1985, when it was founded. To source all of its Conservation Grade grain (about 15,500 tonnes a year), it has contracts with over 100 different farmers. Conservation Grade farms meet the strict environmental guidelines laid down by the Guild which, for example, stipulate that farms must commit at least 10% of their crop area to managed wildlife habitat, minimise the impact of any farm chemicals used and encourage in-field biodiversity. Farmers who adopt the scheme undergo intensive training and their performance is verified annually.

Down on the farm, it's not just the wildlife that benefits; the farmers receive a small premium averaging around 10% above the standard product price. This appeals to many farmers because they are, in reality, getting financial help to achieve standards that will qualify them for other agri-environmental grant schemes such as those run by DEFRA.

Jordans are not the only food producer to use Conservation Grade produce; a number of other food processing firms are also involved and make a variety of products from the grain produced on Guild farms. All processing companies that use these cereals are stakeholders in the scheme and are subject to inspections themselves.

According to Bill, it has, however, not all been plain sailing for the scheme. "With retailer interest in lower prices, some brands have dropped out," he says. He is, however, optimistic about the future. "It is the Guild's intention to encourage more brand owners to become involved and thereby increase tonnages required from Conservation Grade farms."

For further information, please see the Jordans website at:
www.jordans-cereals.co.uk

Chapter 8

SWALLOWS AND AVOCETS FOREVER

Along the shore of Grasmere, one of the jewels of the Lake District, runs a path that lets visitors enjoy views of the lake and the hillsides above. Until recently the path was falling victim to too many tourist feet tramping up and down. Now it has been put back into fine fettle, with money raised by a number of hotels around the lake. Fundraising for the project was spearheaded by the Bridge House Hotel, which raised cash through a voluntary £2.00 opt-in scheme for its guests, most of whom were more than happy to pay up.

The scheme is just one of many run by the Lake District Tourism & Conservation Partnership, which started in 1993 to bring together conservation organisations and businesses engaged in tourism. The aim: to make sure that the resource upon which their livelihood depends is no longer 'loved to death'.

This is not the first time that Lakeland has been threatened by the wrong sort of development. Lest we forget, Beatrix Potter was a highly successful farmer who, with the help of Peter Rabbit, was able to purchase a large slice of central Lakeland and give it to the nation, helping to found the National Trust, our first campaigning body.

It was the Trust's founding fathers and mothers who stopped the despoliation of the lakes by mines, spoil heaps, railways and all manner of other proposed developments, including massive manipulation of the lakes to create a water supply for Merseyside. It's ironic that the creation of one of the major tourist hot spots in the world has, as we have seen, created ongoing problems of its own. If Wordsworth's English Lakes need repair and also constant watch to stop developers getting their hands on them, what of the rest of Britain?

A question of development

As anyone who reads the papers will know, new airports, new housing, new roads – with all their associated infrastructure – are putting the countryside in an ever more precarious position. Of these threats, housing is a particular wriggly can of worms. The Council for the Protection of Rural England (CPRE) say that government studies indicate that up to half a million homes must be built on greenfield land in growth areas of the south Midlands and the south east and east of England over the next 30 years. According to the group, this number of new houses would, in itself, cover an area of some 44 square miles – the size of Newcastle-upon-Tyne.

This is not just a question of land being gobbled up – it also raises other environmental questions. Where will the water supply for all these new houses come from without further damaging water-tables and trout-streams in these regions?

There are many aspects to this complex problem. For example, it is argued that people who own second homes are to blame, driving up prices and so reducing the amount of affordable housing in the countryside. The government has moved to reduce the tax benefits that 'second homers' enjoy, but this alone will not solve the housing crisis that is making rural life increasingly difficult for those on low wages.

What is to be done? Well, I take great heart from the fact that there are many people willing to stand up and say 'no' to developments that threaten to blight the landscape. Some are NIMBYs ("not in my back yard") who simply say no development if it affects them in any way, but many are people and groups who provide creative and pragmatic suggestions on how the needs of rural communities can be provided in the most environmentally-benign ways possible.

Groups such as Common Ground campaign against 'sameness' and 'sub-urbanisation' in the countryside, while groups such as the

CPRE and the RSNC (Royal Society of Nature Conservation, the overlord body of the Wildlife Trusts Partnership) have a task force of volunteers scrutinising planning applications, ready to blow the whistle if they see anything that threatens the countryside. CPRE itself argues that if building must go ahead, then the government should apply a number of environmental 'tests' to all new builds. These would make sure that development would have as little environmental impact as possible, and that the present situation should be used as an opportunity to regenerate 'brownfield' sites, with the development evenly spread geographically (see page 201).

This would help to back up the massive move now afoot – the regeneration of our once-vibrant town centres. Retirees are seeking pads with hospitals, shops and all other amenities to hand. The same goes for single-parent families, who want jobs and houses near schools, crèches, laundrettes, corner shops and good bus services. All can be found in imaginative mid-high-rise schemes that come complete with green space linked to urban walkways and parks. All of a sudden, so-called executive and starter homes developed on suburban or greenfield sites at the end of a maze of already gridlocked tarmacadam are losing their savour. There is also the problem of flood risk in ill-conceived government-backed housing and other developments built on flood plains. Fortunately, insurance companies, ably backed by flood risk maps produced by the Environment Agency, are tackling this.

As I complete the final spell check, the CPRE's latest report has come out rubbishing the most recent government figures and saying there is no need to consider sacrificing any green belt land at all.

An ill wind for the countryside

One area where we are seeing an up-welling of informed protest about development in the countryside is the vexed question of wind power. In recent years – following government targets to save fuel while reducing our nation's release of carbon dioxide – wind farms have become the flavour of a new sort of direct action by politicians desperate to be seen to be doing 'something' for the environment. The current fervour for all things wind has been further backed up by dark warnings about terrorist threats to our future energy supplies. Wind is touted as being really cool for the global greenhouse while breaking our dependency on gas piped in from far away.

To the shame of everyone concerned, local planning regulations have been undemocratically watered-down to speed what can only be termed 'wind blight', as turbines have begun to mushroom across the countryside. Some of the most unspoilt areas of Britain have already been industrialised by the arrival of wind turbines, monstrous industrial developments that open up the countryside to further despoliation, with towers and whirling blades reaching up to more than 300 feet, with even bigger ones in the planning pipeline.

The pro-wind lobby are still trying to shrug off protests against this despoliation of some of the most beautiful stretches of our uplands and coastlines as the whingeing of a vociferous minority of NIMBYs. However, as I write this, the country is rapidly coming to its senses. Hard facts are now in the public domain, showing that the intermittency of wind means that even the best-planned wind farms only produce small amounts of highly-fluctuating electricity, averaging less than a quarter of their installed capacity (Department of Trade and Industry figures 2003). People are asking questions, such as how do you boil a kettle, run a hospital or sustain the National Grid when the wind isn't blowing? What is more, they don't like the answers. Even the German wind and nuclear giant RWE says that however many wind turbines are commissioned not a single conventional or nuclear power-station will be able to be closed down. Indeed, the wind factories across the world have not led to the closure of a single mainstream power-station. It would be an outrage against common sense, engineering, scientific advice and democracy to continue along the path of wind energy without first undertaking an exhaustive and independent cost-benefit study.

The fact is that they are not wind farms but highly inefficient wind factories, some dwarfing Big Ben, that come with permanent giant reinforced concrete foundations, roads that have to take a 50-tonne lorry and new grid lines and pylons. And who is expected to pay for all of this high-rise junk that can do little or nothing to cool the global greenhouse effect or provide a sustainable grid supply? The answer is the consumer, tax-payers and their countryside. The Department of Trade and Industry blandly states that if the government's first renewable energy target is met, it will cost the consumer more than one billion pounds a year in one of the cleverest stealth taxes ever invented.

Add to this the actual costs of wind, in terms of the tens of thousands of birds and bats the wind turbines will kill and the negative impact they will have on tourism, house prices and animal and human health. No wonder more and more people are demonstrating good environmental sense by saying 'no' to wind and asking for more money to be ploughed into real solutions, such as energy efficiency, that really work in economic and environmental terms.

The importance of informed public pressure cannot be over-estimated; it is the mechanism by which good development can be championed and new rural services – from public transport to local schools – can be lobbied for and won.

This, of course, highlights the importance of good information and debate – as we've seen in previous chapters, scientific research, without fear or favour, can provide us with the information we need to decide what is best for our countryside – whether it be genetically-modified crops, the environmental impact of conventional farming (and its economic ramifications) or whether lambs, deer, grouse, bikers or walkers have the right to do their thing within the moorland economy of upland Britain.

I strongly believe that the more people get to know about the countryside and the more they understand how it works and how all the 'bits' fit together, then the work that so urgently needs to be done to restore the balance of our environment can move ahead, free of the debates and infighting that, so often, are caused by misunderstanding and misinformation.

A working countryside

Jobs are, of course, the other big issue in the countryside, with many current policies forcing people out of work, rather than creating much-needed employment for those who want to live in and contribute to the countryside.

So what is to be done? Indeed, what should be done? Should not the countryside 'community' be left to 'market forces' to reshape? Is there actually anything wrong with a countryside that is simply a place most people visit and few people actually live and work in?

The answer draws together many of the themes of the rest of this book – including the central challenge of how the management of the countryside will be paid for. We have seen how the market for food and for the other services that the countryside provides – most notably an environment that tourists can enjoy – is being harnessed, with the application of good science and pragmatic controls well-laced with good old common sense to provide a way of financing conservation and driving the economic restoration of the countryside forward.

As I travel and meet people working in rural Britain, I am finding again and again that projects combining good land management with good financial sense are providing a focus and an employment life-line for rural people; both those who want to be allowed to continue to do the 'right thing' and those who want the benefits of living in the countryside and a chance to help stitch it back into a more natural working order.

Wherever I go I find more and more people engaged on exciting personal, family, or local projects that are all to do with bringing – as many of them have described it to me – real 'quality' back into the picture. Indeed 'quality' is a watchword of Bourne Leisure, whose caravan parks give four million people holidays every year (see pages 141 and 193 for more details of their work).

It's all beginning to happen out there: from the caravan and camping site owners I meet as part of the British Holiday & Home Parks Association's (BH&HPA) award scheme for good environmental practice, to the butcher who proudly sells me locally-produced 'free-range' sausages when I go down to the local village store, I meet people who have found that investing their personal expertise and enthusiasm in projects that directly benefit their local environment – and economy – is a recipe for success.

You only have to turn on the television to find that many others have noticed this trend, from Rick Stein's *Food Heroes* to Hugh Fearnley-Whittingstall's adventures at *River Cottage* – the value of the distinctively 'local' and 'locality-friendly' and the employment opportunities they offer is being celebrated again and again.

The economics of sustainability

This isn't just parochial day-dreaming either: the money involved is quite staggering. The billion pound turnover of organic agriculture has already been highlighted, as have the potential profits from schemes such as 'Conservation Grade' farming that also link the consumer to good environmental practice in the countryside. Other recent figures point to hill walking and rambling in the UK as being even bigger business – with walkers spending over £6 billion each year and supporting up to 250,000 full-time jobs in England alone.

191

Hunting, shooting and fishing all generate significant rural income and jobs (over 36,000 jobs are dependent on hunting).

Head keeper Charlie Pyrie's inspirational television programmes on working a Highland estate were not only based on the charisma of a real countryman who dared to stand up for his rights, they also got their impact from the fact that gamekeepers do just what their name suggests – they look after game and the economy and ecology of the countryside at the same time. In Scotland alone, 1,500 gamekeepers and stalkers support over 7,200 jobs, bringing in £100 million to the rural economy.

Rural tourism (sustainably managed), organic farming, Conservation Grade farming, integrated crop management and the new 'environmentally-friendly' subsidies promised by CAP reform all have the potential to boost the UK's rural economy in a truly sustainable way, providing a 'quality' landscape along with 'quality of life' for those so employed. Add in the jobs – and free-range game, fowl and fish – produced by gamekeeping, together with the economic benefits of sustainably-managed woodlands and suddenly we see that 'environmental economics' can make sense.

Overall, it is clear that agriculture and recreation based on a working and beautiful countryside is an integral part of the economic backbone of rural Britain, whether in the Scottish Highlands or on the downs of southern England.

In light of the importance of tourism to this same rural economy, many groups are now rolling out exciting initiatives to make sure that tourism is as environmentally-friendly as possible. From the Lake District Partnership we started with (see page 73 for more details) to the amazing 'Green Gym' concept of the British Trust for Conservation Volunteers, which combines keeping people, communities and the land in good heart (see page 207 for details), exciting schemes are popping up all over the country that are helping to make sure that the national tourism industry does not kill but nurtures its own golden goose – the British landscape.

The economics and importance of environmental 'quality' have not been lost on one of the biggest players in the bare-feet-on-the-grass tourism game. Bourne Leisure, which owns about 36 caravan parks across the UK, now works with the Ministry of Defence on the management of Sites of Special Scientific Interest near one of its large parks, Perran Sands in Cornwall (see page 141 for details). This work is being mirrored in other projects that are being pioneered by Bourne parks and local Wildlife Trusts around the country. This ground-breaking initiative is just one example of the company's commitment to environmental excellence at its parks. The reason: "Because our customers demand quality. By looking after the environment we can give it to them."

Research figures from the BH&HPA show that each caravan and holiday home pitch generates a contribution of between £500 and £15,000 a year to the local economy.

This win-win situation, in which good environmental management benefits business and provides jobs is, I believe, at the basis of not only sustainable tourism, but – as we've seen throughout this book – sustainable business in rural Britain, whether it is a pheasant shoot engaged in woodland management, a campsite that is creating new lake environments, complete with fishing, or a farm that is converting to organic agriculture and providing oven-ready meals for self-catering holidaymakers or diversifying into B&B eco-tourism for those who want to come and enjoy our rural heritage on the farm.

Muir Burn re-visited

To take just one example that emphasises this important point, let's look again at the controlled burning of our moors – the age-old method of land management that today helps maintain a diversity of semi-natural open, part heather-clad vegetation in many parts of the countryside. It is this type of countryside that is so beloved by many tourists, and that pulls them (and their money) into many of the poorest corners of rural Britain. The result of well-managed burning of the moor not only brings in the tourist pound, dollar, yen and euro and keeps many different birds, insects and plants thriving, but it also provides skilled and satisfying jobs: farmers, sheep shearers, dry stonewallers, fencers, factors, gamekeepers, estate managers, ghillies, bailiffs, rangers, beaters and flankers. All join the hotel managers and innkeepers in the army of people who rely, in part, on good countryside management for their livelihoods.

Good management of moorland can even leave a sweet taste in your mouth. If you've never tried heather honey, you are in for a treat: it's delicious and a healthful substitute for sugar. For a botanist like me, it comes as no surprise that the best heather moors as far as beekeepers are concerned are well-managed grouse moors, where the heather is burnt regularly to encourage new growth. This type of management controls soil erosion and provides vital habitat for a portfolio of wildflowers that the bees love – and that can be turned into a sweet profit for local apiarists.

For me, a lot of conservation simply comes down to the common sense of being a good neighbour. Interestingly, when this idea is applied to the economic picture, 'being a good neighbour' can go a long way to stop altercations and help often-fragile rural economies to survive and prosper. I particularly like one example from a report by the CPRE, which looked at how local enterprise could help shore up local economies: "A wholesale butchers (two brothers) brought livestock from about 30 local farmers. These animals went to a local slaughterhouse, and the carcasses were returned to their premises. This wholesale business produced sausages, cooked meats, and provided freezer packs. These products were supplied to 21 small shops. In addition the family was running two butchers shops, which were also sourcing other foods such as eggs, vegetables, fruit juices, cakes and preserves, from 24 local producers."

This 'good neighbourliness' works particularly well in tourist areas where local produce is a big draw and where tourists looking for something unique to the region can make another economic contribution to the rural economy. It can extend from neighbourhood shops and their suppliers right up to the supermarket chains – as Booths supermarkets showed recently when they claimed a prize in the BBC Radio 4 Food Programme Awards. Booths sources over 20% of its stock from its four home-base counties – Lancashire, Cheshire, Cumbria and Yorkshire – and runs many promotions based on local produce.

If rural businesses can grab hold of the potential for profit in a well-managed countryside hotching with local produce and buzzing with biodiversity, then the rural economy will really have firm 'sustainable' roots. Add to this the potential for 'home working' which could really take off if sufficient funding was made available for broadband internet connections to reach deep into the countryside as it is already doing in far-flung places like the Isle of Lewis. An on-line rural renaissance with many more people working (and not just resting after a hellish commute) in the countryside would be possible.

The rural renaissance

I firmly believe that this rural renaissance is under way – all over the country individuals, communities and businesses are finding ways in which to become guardians of their countryside by putting it back into good heart. With good science, we are finding the right answers to the 'how' of countryside management. With consultation and a 'bottom-up' strategy for environmental management and restoration, we are seeing people pulling together to do the hands-on work needed. Through a new type of business thinking that puts environmental quality at the centre of it, allowing the consumer to know that their choices are making things better in the countryside, we are tapping into a potent engine for positive change.

The pieces of a jigsaw are slowly coming together which, when completed, will produce a Britain bursting with biodiversity, while providing the people of this country a diversity of home-grown food, amazing places to visit and enjoy and vibrant, exciting communities in which to live and work, and quality time at home, work and play.

Why do I think like this? Well, I grew up in wartime London with Arthur Ransome's books, starting with *Swallows and Amazons*. Each one was a window onto what is now an almost-forgotten world. Three of the books that followed on had a conservation theme. *Coot Club* and *Big Six* set on the Norfolk Broads and *Great Northern* set in Scotland. They were about the common sense of free range children, children on holiday who actually did something about helping the local wildlife that was, even back in the twenties, threatened by harmful changes. My dream is that my children's children will be able to follow in their footsteps.

PARISH PUMPS AND SACRED SPACES

Before the days of taps and piped water, the parish pump was the place of daily communion, where local people met to celebrate the gift of potable water and to talk of their joys and sorrows, hopes and fears. Carrying water was a daily task of living, which helped keep muscles and joints active and minds alert, slowing the march of old age and what we now call lifestyle syndromes. Like the church, the pump was an epicentre of a community of souls, bonding them together and keeping them informed and primed ready to solve problems and seize opportunities. The same is true of mosques, synagogues, temples and most of them were founded near holy springs or wells that pre-dated the pump.

To celebrate the Bi-millennium, the Conservation Foundation supplied cuttings from ancient yew trees that are believed to have been growing in what are now churchyards for over 2,000 years. The result was astounding, with special distribution services held in many different venues from cathedrals to agricultural colleges, glebe land to open fields.

Every denomination and faith was represented and the trees were planted in the heart of over 6,000 communities across the length and breadth of Britain.

There was already much good news to report, for many churchyards are managed as nature reserves and local schools help in their maintenance while brushing up on local history, both natural and people-made.

However, many people said, "We cannot just leave it there, what can we do next?" So they became 'parish pumps' in effect: local environmental representatives at the heart of a greener community of souls. David Shreeve, who masterminds the whole scheme explains. "Our aim is to provide information and news to our parish pumps so they can pass this on to their local community. We believe it is also important for the parish pumps to meet one another and they do this at workshops which we organise in association with the Church of England and help from a DEFRA grant.

"Each workshop is hosted by a local bishop and the agendas are drawn up by local people and involve presentations by representatives of local authorities and environmental groups. The day-long events are for people of all faiths or no faith. One recent workshop in Leicester was designed to be inter-faith, as the one common factor shared by the various religions is a concern for the environment. The workshop was held in a church shared by Methodists and Baptists, and the lunch was donated by the Hindu temple across the road. Muslims and Buddhists also took part."

The parish bounds are enormous: the Church of England alone is one of our largest landowners (12,887 parishes at the last count), whose land includes churchyards, vicarage gardens, farms and even forests in a portfolio of hope. Add all the other landholdings of the ecumenical forum in these islands and the total of what are surely sacred spaces is very impressive.

Already, the Church of England is, through its Arbory Trust, allotting parcels of land for use as sites for woodland burials. The land will be consecrated and those who wish to can become part of new woodlands of native plants, shrubs and trees in the branches of which the dawn chorus will be raised on high.

For more information, visit the website at:
www.conservationfoundation.co.uk

THE CAMPING AND CARAVANNING CLUB

The year is 1901. Four Edwardian gentlemen ride their bicycles to Wantage. They spend a pleasant summer weekend camped beside a stream in a watermeadow. In the evening around the campfire, they talk of the pleasures of camping, of outdoor life in the British countryside, and they resolve to form a club, a camping club.

More than a century later, that club is still going strong. It has four hundred thousand members, all active campers in caravans, motorhomes and, of course, tents of every conceivable size and design.

Today it's called the Camping and Caravanning Club and although it has grown into a £25 million business, with nearly 100 of its own sites all over Britain, it's still very much a club owned and run by its members – the campers.

Now the Club is the largest organisation in the world catering for all kinds of campers and caravanners. It's intensely proud of its history, but deeply dedicated to giving today's camper exactly what he or she wants. As well as the Club's own sites, there are more than 1,200 small farm sites, set up exclusively for Club members who want to get away from it all to a quieter corner of the British countryside.

As an organisation that gets all of its pleasure from the British countryside, the Club fully understands its responsibilities in looking after that countryside – giving something back. A network of volunteers, the Countryside Care movement within the Club, organises weekend and holiday projects, all with an environmental or conservation theme.

These are often on nature reserves or in similar locations. For over 25 years, one of the Club's Countryside Care groups has been working with the local Wildlife Trust at Rutland Water, keeping the nature reserve there in tiptop condition.

Another example is on the National Trust's Kingston Lacy Estate in Dorset, where as well as the usual projects of coppicing, footpath maintenance and cleaning out muddy waterways and ponds, Club volunteers have also carried out a massive ongoing comprehensive plant survey.

The Club's own sites too seek to offer camping in an environmentally-friendly way. The *Guardian* newspaper asked recently whether the Camping and Caravanning Club site in Windermere is "the greenest campsite in Britain?" With a landscape developed using local building materials and heavily planted with local species, with rainwater harvesting, sun tubes, waterless urinals and much, much more, the answer may well be 'yes'. The fact that the site provides excellent facilities for backpackers and their families is an added extra.

All of those sites, large and small, bring money into the neighbouring economies. It's reckoned that each family camping on a site adds just under £75 per day to the local economy, and that each six pitches contribute one job to the local community. Add to this the fact that a well-designed site is far less intrusive into the local landscape than most other developments, such as hotels.

Good campsites, like the countryside in general used to be, are places of grass, flowers, trees, bird song and the buzz of insects.

Club members still gather on site to talk in the evening. Today it's more likely to be around a barbecue than a camp fire, but the conversations that have echoed down the century are still the same: "There's nothing to beat camping as the way to enjoy the British countryside."

For more information, visit the website at:
www.campingandcaravanningclub.co.uk

CPRE AND THE GREEN BELT

People in Britain used to only talk about the weather, now a main topic of conversation is the housing market. Unfortunately, unless something is done, this is one 'bubble' that could blow up and burst with dire consequences for the environment, especially in the south east of England.

The government's most recent planning review has suggested doubling the number of new homes that are built each year, which means an extra 120,000 homes a year. According to those in the know, this could place over 8,000 hectares of countryside at risk every five years. It gives yet another push to the government's plans for huge 'growth areas' in the south east of England.

The argument is that there is a shortage of houses and that anyone who wants to stop the house builders is a 'NIMBY' who has no concern for the homeless.

Fighting this preconception are organisations such as the Campaign to Protect Rural England (CPRE) who argue that opening up greenfield sites will do little to ease the housing crisis, but will do a lot to cause a crisis in the countryside. "Relaxing planning constraints to permit additional greenfield development will not lead to more affordable housing, because the market tends to supply larger, more expensive homes on such sites," explains the CPRE spokesperson, Nick Schoon.

Ask any single-parent family or retiree and the needs they single out are jobs, schools, hospitals and other social services near at hand, not at the end of a grid-locked car journey. Community is the other thing in great demand and, for many people, the new-style walled garden suburbs do not provide this. It is clear to me that we should be doing a lot more to follow the example of many other countries around the world and create more urban communities with low to mid-high-rise,

201

all set about with community gardens – examples of good practice lauded in most architectural magazines. Instead it seems that we just get more walled suburbs with slit trench so-called garden plots that do not have enough room to swing a compost heap in, let alone hang up a windchime without annoying the neighbours.

According to the CPRE, the government needs to use the planning system to reuse previously developed, or 'brownfield', land, get away from wastefully low housing densities and secure a higher proportion of affordable housing as part of a planned housing provision. The group argues that good land use planning is the unsung hero of environmental protection – as well as usable, affordable housing in urban areas – and it is lobbying and campaigning hard to make this happen. "Through our national 'Communities not Concrete' campaign, we are calling for the government's housing proposals to be delivered in the most sustainable way for communities across the whole country," Nick explains.

This campaign is backed up on the ground by 'Sprawl Patrol' which puts pressure on council planners to properly implement existing official government planning guidance for developing new homes that already prioritises higher density housing and the use of derelict wasteland over the development of our country's green fields. For example, in Kent the local CPRE group is working to reduce the environmental impact of the draft strategy for the development of Ashford, and nationally the group is doing the same for the study of potential development along the M11 corridor and the strategies for the development of Milton Keynes and the south Midlands.

Sir Max Hastings, President of the CPRE, recently underlined the importance of people standing up against the worst excesses of planning madness, in the *Sunday Times*. "What is a NIMBY except a person who takes a passionate interest in what is being done to his or her community?" he wrote. "In a sane world, a NIMBY would be recognised as a model citizen. The people who invite scorn are those who don't care, don't fight and don't protest when building projects are announced that will transform, and sometimes destroy, the very landscape in which they live."

Alongside this fight to stop the worst excesses of planning from covering communities in concrete, the CPRE is also fighting a more insidious menace: blandness. "What we are witnessing is a levelling down of England. Some landscape character loss is spectacular, such as that left in the wake of new out-of-town ring-road developments," says CPRE's Policy Director, Neil Sinden. "Some is more gradual. Year by year, distinctive hedgerow patterns break up and disappear as land management practices change. One by one, utility transmission masts and poles disturb treasured views. The net effect is a frightening sense that everywhere is becoming the same."

To stop this creeping blight, groups around the country are surveying England's market towns and the countryside around them to catalogue and celebrate their unique local character and distinctiveness.

Working with local councils, groups like CPRE in Shropshire and Lincolnshire are also developing guidelines on issues as diverse as urban development and hedgerow management. These partnership projects should put some flesh on the bones of the campaign and help ensure that at least some bits of the English countryside are allowed to keep their character. Let's hope they succeed, for while we can't all live in Bourton-on-the-Water, surely we should be able to distinguish our homes by a lot more than a number? That rhetorical question, "How did they get it right in the old days?" must not be followed by "How do they get it so wrong in the twenty-first century?"

For more information, visit the website at: www.cpre.org.uk

VIBRANT VILLAGES ARE VITAL

Finding ways to make country living work

Although many suburban and urban people like to escape to the countryside because it is the 'middle of nowhere', on a day-to-day basis rural isolation can be a real problem, especially if you are elderly, infirm or have a family with children who need to be ferried about.

Unfortunately, the steady erosion of rural services such as public transport, shops and places where people get together and meet – churches, chapels, village and school halls, post offices, shops and pubs – has only helped to further isolate people who work and live in the countryside. Now, around the country, rural communities are starting to fight back by finding innovative ways to get the services they need to make life in the countryside practical and more enjoyable. Many have benefited from a really hands-on scheme run by the Countryside Agency, called Vital Villages.

For example, thanks to encouragement and funding from the scheme, villagers in North Lincolnshire have teamed up with the local council to launch a number of dial-a-ride schemes, covering all the parishes in the area. "These are very rural areas with a lot of elderly people," says Angela Hamilton, who manages the project. "Unfortunately, public transport isn't brilliant – it's just not cost-effective to run buses in places like this." The scheme, which is aimed at anyone without easy access to a car, from the elderly to the mother stuck at home with small children, has been a great success. In its first three months, the new service carried almost 1,400 passengers, 76 with wheelchairs.

Rural transport is just one of the key areas that the Vital Villages programme has focused on. It has also provided help with community services such as playgroups, shops and village halls. However, it is about more than just bricks and mortar – it is also about how to help glue communities back together.

North Frodingham in East Yorkshire was, until recently, a village with a problem. "We had three big pig farms," explains local resident Joy Harris, "which were moved out by the government ... so we were then an ageing village population with a big hole in the centre, which was filled very quickly by an influx of new people." As in many rural communities, this resulted in problems of the 'Them' and 'Us' variety. This all-too-common situation spurred the parish council into action. With a grant from the Vital Villages programme, they got a detailed study done on what villagers really wanted for their village – and the things they did not like. To help devise this 'parish plan', the village also held an open day with a model of the village on display. Everyone came in and stuck a flag in it with their views and news.

The future for North Frodingham now looks decidedly rosier, with a number of well-thought-out projects to improve the facilities villagers can enjoy. Community spirit is much improved, for everyone is in the know about what is happening and so there is a sense of common purpose. "We've certainly achieved our original objective, which was to reintegrate the village," says Joy. "And there's now a strong community feeling that came from all the spin-offs."

Overall, the success of the Vital Villages programme has far exceeded everybody's expectations. Sadly, it has now closed to new applicants for funding. However, the Vital Villages teams are now concentrating on helping communities benefit from funds already committed to them. They are determined to share the best practice learnt as widely as possible and get successful approaches (such as parish plans) mainstreamed into regional and local delivery bodies, as recommended by the government's Rural Delivery Review.

Since it was started, the scheme has supported more than 900 parish plans, and awarded 1,100 community service grants and over

1,000 transport grants. As the Countryside Agency itself says: "It's clear that the programme has struck a chord, with many rural areas struggling through lack of amenities and investment. Communities across England have risen to the challenge and seized the opportunity to make real changes for themselves in a very vital way. Their experiences can help others help themselves."

For more information, visit the website at:
www.countryside.gov.uk/vitalvillages
or contact your rural community council for local advice.

GREEN GRAFT? NO, GREEN GYMS!

Healthy people, healthy planet!

You can check in most exercise or diet books to see how many calories running or swimming burn off, but have you ever seen an exercise regime that does the same for tree planting, digging or dry stonewalling? BTCV (the British Trust for Conservation Volunteers) has been working hard to put balance back in our countryside for over 40 years. For the last decade they have been combining exercise with environmental conservation in their Green Gym* project.

The first one I helped to open was in Belfast, where it was great to see a cross-section of local people, from youngsters to those best called age-stressed, exercising arthritic joints and minds back into more active health as part of a caring sharing community. Many had joined to get a bit of camaraderie and, for them, loneliness became a thing of the past. Overall, it was my considered opinion that the improvements in all-round outlook on life brought about by the project were fantastic.

With the tag-line 'Well-being comes naturally', the scheme offers people of all ages the opportunity to improve their fitness by getting involved in practical conservation activities such as planting hedges, creating and maintaining community gardens, improving footpaths and even dry stonewalling. And yes, it does tell you which is best for your waist line – according to BTCV, tree planting and digging both burn off more calories per minute than aerobics or cycling, with the added plus that you can stand back and look at all the good you and your friends have done to both the environment and yourselves.

The BTCV Green Gym scheme has been enthusiastically embraced by many people around the country, a large percentage of whom would not normally have got involved in practical conservation. "I went to the health centre ... and saw the Green Gym advertised, and thought, 'Wow!'" says one Green Gym convert, in explanation as to why they got involved. "Two birds with one stone – getting a bit healthier and conserving the environment as well. It seemed like a good idea to me, so I joined up."

BTCV Green Gyms (as I write there are more than 100 around the country) are open to people of all ages and from all walks of life. People can join for an hour or more on a weekly or twice-weekly basis and are given expert instruction that takes into account their fitness needs and capabilities. Where appropriate, BTCV helps people set up Green Gym community groups. Local BTCV staff provide training and support so that local people can develop their skills and confidence in order to run the scheme themselves. Ongoing support is provided through BTCV's Community Network.

The scheme is just one innovative way in which the BTCV has been encouraging hundreds of thousands of people to get involved with practical conservation in the UK. On any given day, BTCV teams are out helping to put the countryside back into working order. If you haven't had a go, you are missing out on wonderful experience – full of camaraderie and interesting activity and guaranteed to give you fond memories and that warm feeling of having done something 'worthwhile'.

Because it owns no land, BTCV has a unique focus on people and offers training so that people can learn the skills they need to play their part in what is really the UK's conservation corps. Indeed, that is what it was called almost 45 years ago when I was, by accident, part of their first ever project clearing invasive scrub on Box Hill in Surrey to allow orchids as studied by Charles Darwin to thrive in open grassland.

The BTCV Green Gym underlines just how everyone can benefit from helping the environment. The scheme has been the subject of two independent studies by the Oxford Centre for Health Care Research and Development at Oxford Brookes University. These studies have shown that taking part in regular Green Gym sessions can improve cardiovascular fitness and therefore reduce the risk of heart disease and stroke. Of course, digging out ponds and 'scrub bashing' also increases people's strength, but beyond this it also gives individuals a unique and important way of contributing to their local communities – and a wonderful way to meet new friends and have a great time outdoors while learning good old natural history. If you have a problem, personal or environmental, BTCV Green Gyms can help fix it.

Green Gym is a trademark.

For more information, visit the website at: *www.btcv.org*

LOCAL FOOD NETWORKS

Linking farmers with consumers

If you like the taste of local seasonal produce fresh from the fields, then give three cheers for the work of the Soil Association. This ground-breaking group has not only pioneered the certification of organic food in the UK, but also works to link the people who grow and supply food in environmentally-friendly ways with the people in their local area who want to buy and eat it.

Over the last few years, the group has worked to promote and support the development of the local food sector through the now completed 'Food Futures' programme. Through the programme, they have helped local communities secure funding, network and join forces to work together to develop sustainable local food economies. Over 160 different organisations and 1,600 people were directly involved in Food Futures partnerships which generated a wide range of local action.

In Yorkshire, for example, the scheme helped inspire the creation of three new farmers' markets in Heckmondwike, Halifax and Hebden Bridge. In Norfolk, it supported the publication of a local food directory, while in East London, it encouraged the Organic Lea Valley group to take over derelict allotments to grow organic produce for local people. £45,000 a year was secured to support local food projects and to fund a local food development officer.

The Soil Association works to back and inspire local action. "With local food initiatives, ownership is very important," says the Association's Amanda Daniel. "When we work really well, the people involved lead the process. We are there to support them."

The Soil Association has helped in this way all over the country – in Dumfries and Galloway a community garden scheme has been set up to supply a local café, and in Powys a local food marketing campaign has produced car and shop window stickers to spread the slogan 'Are you getting it locally?' Farm shops, farmers' markets, organic food box schemes, local shops – all have been inspired and helped by the scheme.

The Soil Association's current work builds on the foundations laid by Food Futures. The current Local Food Works project is a partnership between the Soil Association and the Countryside Agency. It works with farmers, growers, community groups, local authorities and others and gives practical help, advice, training and guidance to get schemes off the ground and make sure that they prosper.

One of the current priorities for the group is to get organisations such as schools to buy and serve more locally-produced healthy food. Each year, "1.8 billion pounds is spent on food in public procurement for places such as schools and hospitals," says Amanda. "We are encouraging and supporting such organisations to increase the healthiness of their menus and the amount of local, sustainably-produced produce."

For the Soil Association, the current situation in Britain's fields makes the work of promoting local food more vital than ever. "In the wake of BSE and recent food scares, more and more questions are being raised concerning the future of British agriculture," says Amanda. "People are asking where the food on their plate has come from."

Health and the environment are not the only issues of concern to the Soil Association – the local economy is also vitally important. The group points to a piece of research carried out by the New Economics Foundation, which showed that spending £10 in a local organic box scheme results in a £25.90 investment in the local economy. This is because most of the money received for the food is re-spent locally; this money is then re-spent locally again, which gives a vital multiplying effect. Spend £10 in a supermarket, the same report says, and invest only £14 locally.

Thanks to the support of the Soil Association and the hard work and dedication of groups and individuals around the country, more and more local economies are benefiting from this 'local food' effect. Without doubt, thanks to their effort, fresh locally-produced food is now firmly on the agenda and is becoming more easily available than ever before.

For further information, please see the Soil Association website at:
www.soilassociation.org

FAR GRANGE PARK

A caravan country park!

It's not many businesses that can say they have a country park on their premises – much less that they have helped to create it. But that's just what one caravan park owner in East Yorkshire can claim.

Hard work, dedication and a vision of creating a 'better holiday' spurred the owners of Far Grange Park to think big when it came to habitat creation. They have created a 70-acre country park to enhance the holiday experience for their guests and the locals.

"Where our caravans are placed it is quite developed, so it was difficult to plan in a large area of green. We thought that the country park would be a great way of doing this," explains park owner Mike McCann. To develop the site, which was previously pretty boring farmland, the park management created a six-acre lake, put in over 60,000 trees and developed reed-beds, a marsh area and a network of footpaths. There is also an excellent visitor centre to show people what they can expect to see. This is open to both park visitors and local schools.

"All of sudden it has become an oasis for wildlife," says Mike. "As the trees have been planted and hedges allowed to grow wider, we have seen the number of types of birds seen by visitors climb to an average of 60. The occasional visitor's list often tops 80."

The work at Far Grange shows just how restoring and protecting the environment can be good for business. "It's been very well received, it helps us retain customers and impresses people who come to visit," says Mike.

In 1968, Far Grange was a mixed farm with a small dairy herd. A few tents and the occasional caravan would be pitched for the equivalent of 30p a night. The decision to diversify was taken in order to get an additional source of income. The subsequent decision to create the country park was made to improve the quality of the holiday experience for guests as well as to help improve the area for wildlife.

That's not the end of the story at Far Grange. An adjacent golf course has been bought and is now being managed to promote wildlife. All the borders within the park are fringed by wide wildlife boundaries rich in nectar and berry-bearing species and there is a lot of inter-planting between pitches. Thanks to this approach, there are a good number of wildflowers, birds, butterflies, bees and other insects throughout the site. Hares and other grassland species have also been found and water voles are present in the lakes.

Although Far Grange has gone for the 'think big' approach, Mike believes there are opportunities for habitat creation in even the smallest sites. "You don't need a big area to make valuable habitat, you can use a boundary hedge," he says. "Make it nice and tight to stop magpies entering and you'll get lots of little birds visiting. Once you get the habitat right, it's amazing what comes to the fore."

For further information, please see the Far Grange website at:
www.fargrangepark.co.uk

Postscript

LOOKING FORWARD

SHOULD THE BRITISH COUNTRYSIDE BE AT THE HEART OF GOVERNMENT CONSERVATION POLICY AND A SUSTAINABLE ECONOMY?

What is it that makes Britain profoundly different from the rest of Europe? – Our countryside. Why is it that when climate is taken into account, any typical acre of Britain is more biodiverse than any comparable hectare of our partner members in the EU? – The intrinsic character of our countryside. What is therefore the single most important defining environmental policy pre-requisite for Britain in the twenty-first century? – The conservation of the countryside.

The still-enduring character of the British countryside, a jigsaw landscape of individual acres all set about and networked with solar-powered hedges, dry stonewalls and real-time paths rather than a gridiron of standardised, characterless hectares, is under severe threat. This landscape, which allows an intricate mix of farming, commons, woodlands and wilder estates is a multipurpose, multi-coloured pleasant land in which the activities of the farmer, factor, gamekeeper, local poacher and urban dweller can all be sustainably accommodated. Footpaths allow free but directed access, welcoming the townies to download knowledge of how it all works as they ramble and rest. It is this special character and relationship that has, until recently, linked the vast majority of our urbanised population to bite-sized food production, nature conservation and field sports, and inspired a nation proud of the traditions of its rural shires.

Little wonder then that no other part of Europe has anything like the numbers of organisations representing the aspirations of literally millions of people across the political spectrum, all rooted in the worship of the countryside, such as the National Trust, RSNC, the Wildlife Trusts, RSPB, YHA, WI, CPRE, Ramblers' Association, Camping and Caravanning Club, and a plethora of other organisations concerned with recreational use and the proper management of our countryside. This unique situation is no accident, having erupted out of the dark satanic mills and been given life by the accessibility and amazing diversity of the British countryside. As Winston Churchill put it, a countryside which is "something worth dying for".

The conservation of this distinctively different countryside heritage should therefore sit at the heart of the environmental policy of any British government and must be one of the main goals of not just conservation, but also of sustainable economic management and development. Although Britain shares many elements of common heritage with the Republic of Ireland, it differs in one profoundly important context – the way our countryside has been conserved and development planned since the end of the Second World War. Up until very recently, the British countryside was incredibly more biodiverse than that of Ireland (and indeed many other European countries, such as Germany and Holland) because it had been carefully nurtured for centuries, then rigorously protected from inappropriate development by a focused planning system.

This unique approach, both adopted and adapted by successive governments, has recently suffered from a seemingly inexorable and depressing change, and a profound divorce of things of the town from things of the country. This flies in the face of the principles of the founders of the town planning movement such as Howard, Morris and Unwin and has been wrought by the thoughtless rush to standardise political response and impose the will of the few on the many.

Some examples of the problem

In recent years, the ecological disaster of the Common Agricultural Policy has inflicted shameful damage on our intrinsically different heritage by ignoring the fact that Britain does not share a 'common' rural landscape with the majority of Europe and cannot therefore be managed by 'common' rural policy instruments. Two of the key challenges for British environmental policy must hence be to:

i) enlighten and, where necessary, strengthen planning policy and legislation, in order to place a greater emphasis on nature conservation and the preservation of regional and often minutely local intrinsic landscape character; and

ii) radically reform the way in which European rural policy is applied to Britain, making it much more sensitive to our special circumstances, recognising and hence celebrating '*la différence*'.

An example of the folly of so-called environmental policy instruments that fly in the face of the 'common sense', let alone conservation, of our countryside (and hence undermine its biodiversity and beauty) is the government's recent liberalisation of wind farm planning procedures. The global environmental jury is still out (but becoming increasingly sceptical) on the macroeconomic and conservation benefits of wind farms and wind power in general, yet the government is seeking to allow subsidised carnage of our countryside in the pursuit of narrow and dogmatic policy on renewable energy.

Three of our Institutes of Engineering and the Royal Academy of Engineering have all warned that wind farms cannot answer the problem of running a grid to supply the sophisticated demands of a developed country that cannot cope with the risk of intermittency of supply. Engineers of RWE, the German giant of wind and nuclear power, warn us that however many wind farms we build, we still need conventional power-stations to provide the necessary back-up. All must be kept in repair and at least 80% in uneconomic and polluting 'spinning reserve'. Why should the tax-payer, duped by renewable energy spin, foot the bill for destroying much more than the visual amenity of our countryside to build monuments to 'wasted wattage'?

217

We are seeing a similar lack of common sense and care with GM crops. There is a growing body of evidence that shows they are potentially economically and environmentally unsound over the long term, yet they are being forced onto an unwilling countryside in an attempt to arrive at some form of global conformity. The development of GM crops is aimed at reducing the costs of production by reducing the need for inputs. Simple economics determine that, in a competitive market, this will lead to a reduction in market price. Only the most 'efficient' farmers survive in this market-place. The result is bigger, more capital-intensive, labour-diluted, biologically and visually-sterile agricultural businesses. These businesses are not 'farms' in the sense we would understand, they are 'production units' not contributing to the diversity of the British countryside because they cannot, by economic definition, be diverse. This future is profoundly incompatible with a countryside brimming with individual character.

A nineteenth century German economist, Friedrich Engels, spelt all this out in the only really incontrovertible law of economics – Engels' Law. Herr Engels observed that, as economies grow, the share of agriculture in the total economy declines. Prices for food do not rise, as people do not buy any more potatoes or radishes as they get better off, they buy luxuries. The only way for the modern farmer to keep in the 'BMW bracket' is for him to constantly seek expansion. To get bigger he must adopt new technology quicker than his neighbours, forcing them out of business and buying their farms. This is the story of British agriculture under the CAP. It has now been destroying the British (and European) countryside for decades and the adoption of GM technology can only accelerate this.

Neither wind farms nor GM crops are good long-term conservation, or good sustainable business practices. Britain needs to retain and attract the best minds in the world – what better way to do this than to retain the world's loveliest people-managed countryside, easily accessible from our cities and towns and not blighted by millions of hectares of leaden-green, semi-industrialised no-man's or wildlife's land. To avoid an ever-shabbier future, we need a strong rural economy, nurtured and protected by forward-thinking and informed planning legislation that makes the conservation of the character and biodiversity of the countryside a fundamental imperative of the development process.

We boast some of the best town planners in the world and we need to inspire them to set out a sustainable future that links, rather than separates, town and country. The accommodation of John Prescott's additional three million homes into the sort of rich and diverse landscape Britons have the right to enjoy, requires significant and immediate policy change. In a futile, EU-sponsored charge to secure its profitability through industrialised arable and livestock farming, lowland British agriculture is wrecking vast areas of the countryside and confining wildlife to token FWAG (Farming and Wildlife Advisory Group) field corners and wildflower margins. Much of East Anglia is becoming more and more like the North German Plain or the American Mid-West, desertified and running out of water. Is this the type of inaccessible, soulless landscape in which we now want to force over five million British people in their three million new homes to live?

An example of a singularly British approach that has got things right is in our attitude to rivers, the arteries carrying the essential lubricant of a sustainable and healthy economy. Britain leads the world in the control and mitigation of urban water pollution and the management of our rivers and streams is a testament to the care of riparian owners who manage their banks for a diversity of interests, from fishing to agriculture.

The Test and Itchen remain the world's leading trout-streams and the countryside through which they flow is amongst the loveliest and most biodiverse in Europe; all of this the result of responsible, long-term and intergenerational partnerships between private sector landowners and those concerned with conservation. Even in urban Britain we see this approach yielding dividends. The River Thames is the cleanest river running through any capital city in Europe and its most urban tributary, the Wandle, now has both brown trout and salmon back after an absence of over 150 years. The Tyne, in what was once one of the most polluted parts of Britain, is now one of our best salmon rivers and the Tweed now leads the pack in the North Atlantic.

However, the links between the management of the countryside for food, biodiversity and recreation, perhaps exemplified by a clear running trout-stream at the heart of the landscape, are all beginning to founder on the rock of social bigotry. Amongst the most urgent things we need to do therefore is to reconnect the town and the country. This will require a series of policy changes aimed at reconciling what has become an ever-widening gulf of misunderstanding.

One example of this is the anti-hunting bill that lumbered its way through the Houses of Parliament. On one side was the perception that hunting mammals with dogs is cruel, a perception in direct conflict with the other side's firm belief that hunting with dogs is the least cruel means of controlling pests or culling game.

In effect, as I type these final words, the arguments roll on and the government is at least bending to embrace the fact that culling of the right sort is an important part of all land management. The hunting fraternity is also looking to ways of engaging with, not confronting, the general public.

One area where we might make a start is by doing what other countries, such as Germany and the United States, have done through their approach to hunting and game licensing and its relationship with national nature conservation funding. Our own Game Licence is a sham, as it collects minuscule amounts of revenue, costs more to administer than it raises and is widely ignored. If we follow the lead of our American cousins by making field sports participants contribute to nature conservation in a direct and transparent way, we might just get each side to begin to value each other's views and replace the currently charged and bigoted atmosphere in which their current relations take place.

Where to from here?

We need to get the basics right – potable water, healthy food and space for healthful recreation. All of these are a matter of good conservation and responsive, responsible planning, tailored to local ecological, cultural and social conditions.

There are emerging alternative profitable, conventional and potentially widely adoptable systems, such as 'Conservation Grade' farming and development planning techniques based on local 'landscape character'. However, both need a change in environmental and planning policy, taking us away from the contemporary 'one size fits all' dogma of the EU, in order to make a real difference. France and Germany need this as much as we do – we in Britain must therefore take the lead in securing this change by opening and sustaining the debate.

If we get the balance of our approach to biodiversity management right, as we appeared to have done for centuries before the advent of the CAP, both the British and European economies will continue to grow and we can stitch society back together with the enduring twine of environmental common sense rather than the brittle thread of short-term green spin.